"*Raising Free People* is the book that those of us navigating unschooling through a decolonisation and social justice lens have been waiting for. Akilah's straight up rich and honest descriptions and insights on the many highs and lows of living with authenticity and raising free people resonate completely. There are so many 'What? How did I not notice that before?' moments. It is priceless that we get to journey with the Richards as they navigate overcoming their schoolishness and fears about liberation and community, accompanied by the insight, guidance, and encouragement of constantly checking their mindsets to do the inner liberation work to make the outer liberation a reality."
—**Zakiyya Ismail, convener of the Learning Reimagined Unschooling Conference, Johannesburg, South Africa**

"This is an insightful, brilliant book by one of today's most inspiring leaders in the realm of Self-Directed Education. We see here how respecting children, listening to them, and learning from them can revolutionize our manner of parenting and remove the blinders imposed by the forced schooling that we nearly all experienced. I recommend it to everyone who cares about children, freedom, and the future of humanity."
—**Peter Gray, research professor of psychology at Boston College, author of *Free to Learn***

"It's becoming more common for parents to recognize the inefficiencies and irrelevance of conventional schooling and to desire something better for their children. Yet few have had the courage and commitment to forge a new path for their family based on freedom, liberation, autonomy, and love like Akilah S. Richards. Even fewer have been able to share such deep insights and empowering narratives about reclaiming our lives and trusting our children to create their own."
—**Tomis Parker, agile learning facilitator at ALC Mosaic and board member of the Alliance for Self-Directed Education**

T0054153

"Akilah's voice is so warm and personal that sometimes I don't notice how seriously radical and impactful her words are—that is, until I catch myself speaking and listening to my own child with noticeably more humility, curiosity, and respect. *Raising Free People* pulls off that rare miracle: it's a book for everyone, offering fresh and significant insights to people like me who've spent decades learning about unschooling, while simultaneously welcoming and engaging the parent who has never previously stopped to question the validity or importance of school. Akilah's vision is unsurpassed when it comes to drawing the connections between collective liberation and personal freedom. Her clarity on this and similar issues has already deepened the communal wisdom of the Self-Directed Education movement, and I hope that her book reaches millions of parents, so that millions of children may grow up knowing, trusting, and fully inhabiting their own unique gifts."

—**Grace Llewellyn, founder of Not Back to School Camp, author of *The Teenage Liberation Handbook***

"It is uplifting to experience this message delivered with such clarity and in such a practical and inviting manner that it will naturally encourage and draw families to want to take this first step toward living this. I want to thank Akilah for this and encourage any families that are thinking more about learning to raise free adults to jump right in and take this journey of learning with Akilah. Her care, empathy, presence, and insight are at the very forefront of how families can experience living together in a healthy, integrated, and harmonious manner, where learning is an ongoing journey to deepening their connections."

—**George Kaponay, world traveler, storyteller, writer, social entrepreneur, and cofounder of the Family Adventure Academy**

Raising Free People
Unschooling as Liberation and Healing Work

Akilah S. Richards

Raising Free People: Unschooling as Liberation and Healing Work
© 2020 Akilah S. Richards
This edition © 2020 PM Press

ISBN: 978-1-62963-861-4 (hardcover)
ISBN: 978-1-62963-833-1 (paperback)
ISBN: 978-1-62963-849-2 (ebook)
Library of Congress Control Number: 2020934742

Cover by Kris Richards
Interior design by briandesign

10 9 8 7 6 5 4 3 2

PM Press
PO Box 23912
Oakland, CA 94623
www.pmpress.org

Printed in the USA.

Contents

Foreword

On the twenty-fifth morning of March 2020, the year of the pandemic, a billion Indian households awoke to the skin-curdlingly unsettling roars of horned monsters, the kinds that modern legends warned dwelled under the beds of scared little children. These monsters were, however, of a different sort: they were *in* the beds of their children. As a matter of fact, *they were their children*.

"Horned monsters?" you ask. Well, forgive my embellishments, but they might as well have been floating spaghetti heptapods with tentacles for eyes or something far less bizarre. What matters, what my point is, is that those parents must have stared awkwardly at their own kids as anomalous entities, like things squirted out of the twilight zone.

In the wake of the exponential explosion of the novel coronavirus, nicknamed SARS-CoV-2, and following the "social distancing" protocols other nation-states under siege had executed to combat the pandemic, India made the unprecedented decision to shut down its economy. Flights were cancelled. The food production and distribution cycles dried up. Local kiosks were shut down by cane-brandishing police officers. Schools were ordered closed. More than a billion people were ordered to observe difficult lockdown procedures. For most parents, suddenly being at home with their own children during what was normally school hours was an existential crisis that would quickly capture the imagination of the educationally conservative country.

For my wife and me, unschooling parents of our two children, it was Wednesday.

Word travels fast in the electrifying atmosphere of a crisis. We were soon contacted by a journalist from the country's most prestigious daily, and then by another from another daily. Their questions were similar: What do mothers do with their children during the lockdown? Do you have suggestions about exercises to offer or how to keep our children productive?

My wife Ijeoma, an Indian brought up in this bureaucratic culture where the primacy of schooling was as unquestionable as the popularity of cricket, showed me the questions in her inbox. We chuckled at the mainstream anxiety about childhood productivity: our own concerns were often how to escape the unquenchably demanding prolificity of our never-schooled children!

Then, as we are often invited to do, we wondered about our never fully named practice of unschooling and about our own journeys from university lecturers to disillusioned professors dispensing grades to the students we loved.

We remembered the first sky-petaled days of our romantic relationship in Nigeria and the ensuing months leading up to our wedding when we decided that our Indian-Nigerian kids-to-come would be spared the shadows of schooling.

We reminisced about the first time we held our six-year-old never-schooled daughter Alethea—in a small clinic in Chennai, a few minutes after 6:33 p.m., when she was born—and how we came to know with our bones, as her tiny pink grip folded around my index finger, and as her clear eyes sparkled with the power of a warrior princess, that we simply couldn't send her away to the quiet captivity of a desk and predetermined answers.

We discussed Alethea's paintings and poems and our two-year-old son Kyah's transgressive development. We recalled instances when we felt like we were swimming against the tide, when our parents chastised us for denying our children the comprehensive education we had received, and when it felt easier to outsource our children to an anonymous system so troublingly connected to the militaristic motivations of nation-states.

Lingering at the threshold of a "send button," a panoramic vision of our journey flashed before our eyes reinforcing the familiar convictions, old friends we knew; our unschooling journey was a decolonial path of fugitivity. A matter of more than racial justice. A matter of ecological transformation. A yearning beyond the wet dreams of progress and development. A cartographical pilgrimage into the cracks opening in a civilization that never worked for Black and Brown bodies like ours. An intergenerational project that was as lengthy as the Middle Passage, as seditious as the undercommons the "New World" slaves seeded with "Samba" rhythms, with "Santerían" spiritualities, with "Rastafarian" syncretism, with "Gayap" economic principles, and with calypso. Our work was a desire to leave the plantation that produces questions like "But is this the right thing to do?"

When we hit "send" and dispatched our carefully worded responses to those journalists, an invisible thread of kinship and mutual fugitivity connecting us across distances to the prophetic wisdoms of our sister Akilah Richards glowed seductively.

And, yes, Akilah writes, sings, remembers, whispers, spits, screams, cusses, and speaks with the studious and raw eloquence of a prophet. Not someone who predicts the future or lectures about doom, but someone who knows that the *thick now* is richer than the prevailing myths of our time allows us to think. Someone who knows that our children, the invisible ones we must now mount expeditions to meet again, are key to our own manumission.

This book, capably curated with the craftsmanship of a pilgrim mother who stands at a crossroad calling for new paths to be boldly trod, is one in a pantheon of texts reminding us that enchantment is not in short supply. That learning happens everywhere. That this moment, when our children are temporarily released from their incarceration in "studenthood," is a moment of opportunity to study (in the Fred Moten sense of the word) the troubling complicity of mainstream schooling and public education systems with colonialism. That forward movement is no longer possible, and we must go awkwardly into playful paths by allowing our children to lead the way.

There is something endearingly criminal and Robin Hood–esque about Akilah's thesis in this book about raising people. The first time I met her—at an unschooling un-conference in Johannesburg—I could not take my eyes off her and her beautiful family. Akilah reminded me of my dear sister Tito. Kris, Akilah's husband, towered above everyone else at that gathering and did not ring any bells of resemblance, but he certainly reminded me of a certain gentle Kryptonian of popular comic lore.

It was more than familial resemblances that attracted me to Akilah. She spoke with the eloquence of the everyday. She refused to disconnect her quest to understand the architectural injustices of our world from the way she was co-parenting her daughters. Her daughters, Marley and Sage, whose stories shimmer through these pages, were fierce in their independence. I remember being proud of them.

When we were introduced to each other, I heard stories of this wonderful Jamaican-American family of four, their enchanted nomadicity, their experiments in thwarting the deadening effects of modernity, and their inquiry into freedom. Akilah was powerful and direct when she spoke; her power was tucked well within the folds of her calming and unassuming presence. I would later learn about how this Jamaican woman, this once stellar student and brilliant achiever, learned the hard way that no matter how hard she excelled in a system rooted in pain, no matter how strenuously she struggled to cut off her "exotic" edges so she could fit within the expectations of whiteness, the system only got more intelligent in its capacity to dispossess, render invisible, and *background* the bodies of the not yet human.

I would also learn of Akilah's varied experiences, from being manhandled by cops to being otherized on popular television shows. I would learn of her penetrating questions about childhood, about Blackness and liberation, about parenting, about slavery, about colonization—all forged in the waltz and rest of intimate experience not in the luxurious distance of academic expertise.

On her back were the many whip marks of injustices she had suffered. In her belly the microbial worlds still processing the traumatic memories of those stolen from Africa. Those who knew defeat. But there is a hidden power that only defeat knows; there is a power that comes with being buried: just ask the seed. This is the kind of power tricksters claim when they mock the muscling claims of the so-called powerful. And this is the notion of power I remember thinking about when Akilah showed up in Johannesburg, the most embodied living example of a fugitive I had ever come across.

Like Akilah herself, this book—modestly titled—is an invitation to stray away from the fixed algorithms of colonial reinforcements. To know power differently. To refuse the freedom the system offers. To allow the cacophony of noise to draw us away from the beguiling harmony of troubling colonial order.

When Akilah writes that "children are groomed to show up, both at home and in public, in ways that make adults comfortable" and connects this phenomenon to the ways "Black folks in the countries I grew up in, Jamaica and America, have also been groomed to show up in ways that make the people who are in greater positions of power than us ... comfortable," she channels a different notion of Blackness—not the one that fights for an equal piece of a carcinogenic pie, but the one that knows there are other places of power. Other notions of learning. Other ways to figure and perform education.

When she writes about the heady days of Caribbean decolonial sentiments, when it was trendy to adopt an African
name as a way of disavowing the universality of whiteness,
and yet near impossible for the Black population to imagine
freedom outside of the path that leads through school, she
acknowledges that victimhood and a failure of imagination
can trap minorities in the same dynamics they expressly seek
freedom from.

Through the path of unschooling, this book tracks a
journey into the sweltering compost heat of Blackness as
fugitive emancipation, where we might be remade and ren-
dered fit for other performances of freedom. It reminds us
that there is life beyond the intergenerational project of insti-
tutionalized public education. It suggests that children are
not born; they are *constructed*, made. Modernity constructs
children as citizens in the making, as furniture beneath the
all-powerful "adult gaze." Akilah calls this "studenthood" and,
with stories that will hold you in their little pink grip, demon-
strates how this "studenthood" is a racial project of perpetuating the centrality of the human subject, the Euro-American
Enlightenment self that is disconnected from magic and
animacy and the vibrancy of ecology, from the wisdoms that
trees secrete, from the pollination songs that empty space
traffics, from learning-as-becoming, from the miraculous
abundance that is available if we knew how to look. And do
we ever need a sense of abundance now!

As I write this foreword, reported cases of people infected
with the coronavirus have surpassed three million. More
than a hundred thousand people have died. The prospects
of finding a vaccine are getting dimmer and dimmer—since
recovered patients do not seem to be producing antibodies to
keep the disease at bay. The world has changed.

The old normal is dead.

Where I come from, they might say that to find your way
you must become lost. Becoming lost is hard work; it means
we learn to touch the contours of how we found ourselves. It

means we run our fingers gently along the surfaces of our extensive bodies, over our hopes, over our dreams, over our notions of freedom. By doing so, by mapping where we are, fugitive openings might become more obvious.

This book is an opening and a risk. A decolonial journey. Its author, standing at the crossroads with Èsù, the Yoruba god of change, knows the urgency of the awkward. Akilah writes *rudely* and with the lyrical precision of a herbalist whose great task is to bring you to the site of your rite of passage. She hasn't got time, yours or mine. As we would say in Lagos, *she no sen' you.* She is not going to patronize you. Yet her non-proselytizing directness feels like the hard medicine of someone who knows in her bones, in her arm bent behind her back by a traumatized White police officer, in her palm that has just gently slapped her daughter and wondered if she wasn't perpetuating the slavery dynamic of the "adult gaze" and the "good nigger," that we are not free, that we are caught in an assemblage of gestures and behaviors that have confined our imaginations, that we are living out the imperatives of old dynamics—even in our quests to win, to behave properly, to become black billionaires, to earn labels, to beat them at their own game.

I trust this impulse. I think you, fellow sibling in this age of forced fugitivity, might find that as you let Akilah speak, that same invisible neuronal thread, that underground tissue that is enlisting families and parents and children in social isolation into the service of the unschooled awkward, that yarn of undisclosed power, will burn brightly. And you may then know another way.

Bayo Akomolafe
Chennai, India

For KASM Clan,
And for you *same* one, DelRose.
Thank you for choosing me.
Unu done know aready.

Introduction

Good Morning America (GMA), a national morning television product of American-based ABC Television, ran a post on their blog in April 2020, the year I'm publishing this book. The post was an add-on to a video segment in response to the *crisis schooling* quandary that parents found themselves in when a novel coronavirus hit and pushed us into a pandemic. GMA, like many other media at the time, had been addressing widespread concerns about the interruption of standard schooling and the options available to ensure that children still kept up with their studies and academic goals. Quarantines that mandated sheltering in place meant that learning as most people know it would need to happen through creative, virtual means—school at home—because no one was leaving home, let alone sitting in a group with students and staff. The piece was written by a journalist who tried unschooling for *two days* and, as a result, used the platform to explain what unschooling was, how it worked, and if it worked. The problem is that this journalist was not familiar with unschooling, and though she had reached out to me to chat about it, she didn't understand the philosophy. She interpreted unschooling to mean: conduct school at home, have a little more influence over how to frame the information and a lot more room for children to try new methods of taking in information and meeting set-for-them goals.

I never heard back from that journalist after our email and phone chat. I found out about the published piece through a Google Alert (on my name), followed by the numerous mentions and tags I got on Facebook and Instagram from outraged people who had seen the coverage. Unschoolers and self-directed communities rallied, and each said their piece on social media about how much the article misrepresented and how harmful it was during a time when families were scrambling to find viable solutions to the old normal of schooling. Unfortunately, this wasn't the first time someone got excited about the possibility of what unschooling might solve, only to apply a schoolish lens to it. That lens translates unschooling as a curious and *kinda* intriguing educational methodology that gets children to buy into goals determined for them through mandated curricula or beliefs. In this translation, the learner "gets to choose" how, not whether, to study and regurgitate the information they're being required to study. This is not unschooling.

In actuality, many adults have had their own discovery of unschooling, whether or not they've named it. It's usually a result of their own crisis with conventional school. Something disrupts their normal pattern and expectations for their child—grades dropping, behavioral issues, loss of income to support a particular type of schooling, or, in this case, the COVID-19 pandemic—and they latch on to the premise of learning happening at home naturally through life experience. The problem is that they keep all the schoolish elements too, and the resulting approach is not unschooling but more of a Frankenstein-esque version of a wholly natural thing. It can look like learning, but only because we don't understand as a society how learning happens. So this Frankenstein is harmful, in that it can, from a distance, appear similar to a natural thing (learning) but, upon observation, is a bona fide monster, constructed from the cadavers of standardized education notions and the good intentions of the people creating it and not much else. Actual unschooling skills—which we'll discover and dance with all through these pages—are essential services and essential skills. What many families are facing now, as I write this introduction, is not a crisis founded in lack of going to a classroom. No, friend, it's evidence of another pandemic, one where severely underdeveloped social and emotional skills are overshadowed by the performance, competition, and one-upping that schools teach us to value. Much of the stress in homes in my current time ain't got shit to do with learning! It's about adults and children being together all day with no tools for being around each other comfortably for more than a few moments at a time. Tools like healthy conflict and stress management and having to face the open wounds of certain personal challenges, instead of hiding from them.

A working mother's dictator-type parenting style suddenly collides with a stay-at-home dad's more relaxed approach to his children. Suddenly, this is a thing they're having to face seven days a week, instead of just on weekends—with wine . . . and whateva else.

Instead of performing the version of themselves that a young learner usually shows their parents, they dole out the pushback that's usually reserved for their classroom teachers or the younger kids in their school. Since their parents don't know the issues their child is facing, they label it a crisis schooling situation, resolvable only by school at home situations where teachers can "come get their kids" from the frazzled parents.

These are not education issues. They are relationship and community issues. They are a matter of missing life skills, skills that our schools are not designed to support our children in developing but that they—we—still end up needing. We meet that missing-skills reality especially when we are called to show up without our vices and our voluntary social distancing from our homes. When your normal patterns shift unexpectedly, what are the things you remember unlearning about yourself? What did you do for years that became, in almost an instant, unbearable? In those moments, when you realize you want to go down *those* roads, to understand *those* things about yourself, to ask and answer *those* questions, you are experiencing unschooling, because it ain't just about education. It's about learning, which happens in any setting, at any time, without curricula and designated teachers.

As a matter of fact, what if I told you that we all become unschoolers at some point? At some stage in life, we all encounter the unlearning of ideas that are not germane to our particular nature. One might discover, in her forties, that she doesn't actually hate reading; she just spent years as a student reading dense text and reciting it back on tests, with little time for reading that felt pleasurable or even informative. Or one might learn that he cannot, in fact, stay at this "good job" for another two years, because despite its benefits and the validity it brings to his existence, he loathes the industry, despises the work, and feels utterly unfulfilled by how he is spending his energy. As an adult unschooler, I am constantly learning about myself, putting habits and ideas away and claiming or reclaiming others, as a result of my growing understanding of my way of learning and of managing my emotions and relationships. This—not leniency and a really fun curriculum—is what unschooling means and what it facilitates when you learn how to tap into it. It is a literal act—to consciously and logistically remove schools and classrooms as a child's primary space for learning and socializing. More than that, it is an entire approach to life and relationships. In that approach is a constant growing and sharpening of the by-products of anti-oppressive, personally driven learning: self-knowledge and healthy self-determination, safe relationship building, socially just leadership and collaboration, curiosity, and genuine joy.

While we can get those things in ways other than becoming unschoolers, we seldom do, until the lack of those skills has caused enough pain and disruption that we move toward it instead of away from it. We usually have to seek out and learn how to trust and embody those things while we unlearn and discover ways and means to work through what we discover. It can look like going to therapy or quitting a soul-sucking job, leaving a toxic relationship, or deciding to learn how to finally trust ourselves as worthwhile and whole, even when we're being told or shown that we are not (good, smart, rich, pretty, handsome, whatever) enough. Those are life skills. They are tools for having a healthy relationship to boundaries, to conflict, to communication, to life. Those tools are embedded in the thing I know as unschooling, which is far more than merely the act of decentering school. It is a set of practices, some established, many emergent, that help to sustain a lifestyle of trust and respect-based communication. That is what the stories and people inside these pages will bring you. A series of opportunities to listen with your whole self. Sentiments invoked to shift your perspective on power. Stories transformed into tools that might invite you to aspects of your own life gone unexamined, your own school wounds and other hard times cleverly disguised as your parenting style.

In the rest of these pages, you and I will walk together and examine the beautiful mess of unravelings that unschooling ushers in. You might get turned around, triggered, riled up, or experience any one of a myriad of emotions in between. Don't worry, 'cause this isn't the unraveling like the thread on your favorite sweater; it's more like the unraveling of a mystery, like resolving something, like losing the obscurity, like making plain what once was experienced as hidden or beyond reach. To embrace a new lens—a new paradigm, actually—of daily, loosely planned, lived experiences that see and serve learning, a learning that happens when human wisdom is nurtured by people with the skill to understand how learning works, people who have experience with how to lean into self-directedness as a channel for fulfillment, joy, learning, and sustainable relationships with ourselves, each other, and our planet. Here is our chance to act together to resolve a vile situation whereby education and learning got confused for each other and children and childhood got colonized.

CHAPTER ONE

Beginning Our Process from Being Schoolish to Becoming Self-directed

Liberation, aka *getting free*, has always been part of the ongoing discussions happening in my family and community. That's largely due to me being born in the late seventies in the same small country as the visionary who developed one of the earliest documented international movements that wasn't about conquering or converting and was led by someone Black. In 1977, a twenty-year-old music lover living in a coastal city near Kingston had her first baby, me. By then, it had barely been two decades since his designation as our island's first national hero, and the psychological and political ripples of native son Marcus Garvey's efforts were still very much discussed and felt. His unapologetically African callout got everyone's attention, and this deepened awareness around the ways Black people's freedoms were being disregarded or disturbed and heavily influenced the arts in Jamaica. Riveting Rastafarian musicians like Bob Marley and the Wailers and Burning Spear tuned our ears to rhythm and resistance, encouraging people to question everything, to call out injustice, and to make—as noted Jamaican lecturer, dub poet, and popular broadcaster Mutabaruka later put it—"the distinction between education and indoctrination."

Those songs of freedom were being played on speaker boxes that towered atop the ubiquitous and notoriously ragged pickup trucks that the most resourceful among us connected to megaphones and rode around neighborhoods with live, loud-ass, scripted advertisements about political, religious, and social events. This movement was palpable and was evident in art, poetry, music, and policies, even trickling into homes through reexamined approaches to parenting. Names of African origin were proudly given to new babies (like me, Akilah Safiah), while long-standing celebrations of people like Christopher Columbus were outright challenged within academia, as well as in homes. Collective efforts among families to ensure children knew the relevance of Black and Brown people in history was on the rise. The messages around me told me to be Black and proud; I was already Black, and to get proud I would first need a good education. For some families, Black Pride meant that children's studies be extended beyond classrooms, outside the context of the Eurocentric textbooks that told us the real heroes were White men, and that all people of color were *exotic* accent marks in the real and central story of world history. This influenced some Jamaicans to approach life anew, some migrating to other countries for more opportunities to pull themselves out of survival mode. In smaller pockets, some began dressing in traditional West African attire, studying African scholars, writing books, reading then illegal ones (such as *The Autobiography of Malcolm X*), and broadcasting radio and television programs about Black history before the transatlantic slave trade. Education needed to happen outside of school, and more people began to acknowledge this and organize to add to their children's schooling with more education about Africa and Africans.

Many people wanted to know more about the history of African people, and it affected their perspectives about themselves in their current lives. For children in the late seventies and early eighties, though, not much changed in our daily lives. I guess part of that was because for many families school felt like the safest place their child could be while they worked and pondered and provided. We went on obeying our parents and teachers, smiled politely while our adults impressed their friends with our good report cards, our well-mannered ways, and how we wore our Good Studenthood like badges of honor. Education, we knew from being told, was the key to liberation, and it was our jobs as the futures of Jamaica to excel in school, so we could make our families, our country, and, consequently, ourselves proud.

When I moved to America in the late eighties, we landed in South Florida. Jesse Jackson was trying to win a presidential nomination for a second time, and Def Jam, BET, and *The Cosby Show* told us that hard work and good education got Black folks the good, liberated life. Dr. Johnetta B. Cole had recently become the first Black woman president of Spelman College, and a brilliant Black journalist named Oprah Winfrey got her talk show syndicated, and she was on our TV every single weekday! Despite media misrepresentations, Black excellence and liberation were showing up, and our families were all in consensus that the path to this excellence, this route to this liberation, was tucked firmly inside a good education. Just like in Jamaica, I gathered from the messages around me that I could . . . and should be Black and proud—but not if that interrupted being Black and educated. As I started my American schooling, I began internalizing the idea that I had to tuck away my personhood (personality, preferences, opinions, too much Blackness) to excel at studenthood. My elementary school had a predominantly Black student population, but most of our faculty and staff were White, and that's when I began my ongoing understanding of how assimilation shows up in school.

Separate from my observations on *how* my Blackness mattered in America was the way I performed studenthood. There was a performance I regularly coproduced with teachers and other Managing Adults in my life—Honor Roll Achiever, Gifted Student, Winner, Overseer of other students' behaviors—straight A's, straight hair, and a fast disappearing non-American accent—whatever moves it took to win at studenthood. And then there was my actual life—the things I did with my "free" time: writing about my feelings and doing the things I wished I could spend more time doing. Mostly, I spent my days performing intelligence for adults, much like you probably did, in preparation to achieve the dreams applied to me through mandatory lesson plans administered in classrooms, all without my input or consent.

Of course, I didn't think anything of *lack of input or consent* back then. I wasn't particularly special, in that I, like most children, had become skilled at looking occupied or focused and otherwise performing our intelligence to avoid the consequences of apparent mediocrity that adults enforced. And because we believed that doing well in school meant we would do well in adult life, school was the vehicle for liberation. So, like most of us, I began developing coping mechanisms for studenthood; vices that would stay with me well into adulthood. I created these childhood vices to navigate the loss of personal power and lack of consent that was a normalized part of my existence. From elementary through high school, I busied myself: I was captain of this squad, member of that one, vice-president of that student organization, employee at this fast food joint, and contestant of this dance competition. Basically, my coping strategy was doing a shit-ton of extracurricular activities to keep my mind engaged and to practice doing things I liked with my time but, mostly, to distract myself from facing the things that probably—no, definitely—needed to change.

I went on to college in Atlanta, Georgia, and shortly after graduating with a bachelor's degree reconnected with Kris, a high school friend. Together, he and I put our American Dream blinders on and set out to do what any *good* Caribbean child knows she or he is expected to grow up to do: get married, land the good job, live in the impressive house, have the grandchildren, send them to the best schools you can afford. Oh, and praise the Jesus (can't leave that out since we're talking about Jamaicans). We checked nearly all of those boxes. It took nearly seven years into parenting before we realized we were quite possibly unnecessarily stressed and unhappy and changed the direction of our liberation walk. That change looked like withdrawing our daughters from school, selling everything we could sell, giving away the rest, and living as digital nomads for nearly a decade now.

We traded in our Georgia suburb for crashing on couches and renting one-room apartments in different parts of Jamaica. For six years, we spent six or more months a year in Jamaica, where the cost of living was relatively low for us and exploration opportunities were vast and easily accessible. It turns out our daughters took learning *with* them; it didn't happen mainly in schools. They were using the internet to learn languages and meet people who taught them about the games, artists, entrepreneurs, and cultures they chose to study. Their studies didn't look like textbooks and classrooms. They were done in local restaurants, public parks, chance meetings turned regular meetups, virtual chats with people they were teaching English to in exchange for learning their language or tutoring in art. Learning was everywhere, and school was not always the best vehicle to get it. In fact, through conversations with other parents who'd pulled their children out of schools, I realized more and more that school got in the way for many children, and if our communities were more focused on ways to pivot liberation walks away from institutions and toward the leadership of the learners themselves, we wouldn't just solve the countless issues we face in and because of schools, we would change society for the better. Unschooling would become both my family's path away from institutions and toward confident self-governance and personal leadership and a chance to positively affect society.

Our family defines unschooling as a child-trusting, anti-oppression, liberatory, love-centered approach to parenting and caregiving. As unschoolers, the four of us operate with a core belief that children own themselves and that parents and other adults work with children to nurture their confident autonomy not their ability to obey adults' directives. And when education is forced and standardized, it stifles natural learning and the things to which learning inevitably lead, kills creativity, chokes out confident autonomy—it is an act of colonization. We saw it begin to happen with our own children not even a full year into our daughters' schooling, so they (and, eventually, Kris and I) began transitioning out of school almost as fast as they began transitioning into it. But prior to that transition out of school, our experiences as parents of young students found us heavily involved in our daughters' elementary school everythings.

We began as adults determined to help our daughters settle into their individual rhythms of *stellar studenthood*, so that they could eventually be free to do what they want and contribute meaningfully to the world around them. We began as people who believed that our daughters deserved—and we would ensure they got—the best college education they could attain. Along the way, our focus on college was disrupted repeatedly by what we observed. And because of those observations, we went from supporters of good schooling to supporters of Marley and Sage. We went from school to homeschooling, and then to something altogether different, a path these pages will cover in detail. That path was inspired by the simple but powerful practice of spending more time with our daughters outside of their classrooms, outside of the context of student or school.

While we were observing our daughters, which we started doing during that milestone summer break in 2012, we didn't have many "aha" moments. I wasn't immediately seeing how they were learning while not being told what to study. No big "would you look at that" moments that encouraged us to slow down with assignments and tests. What we mostly had were questions; I'll share some of them with you in a minute. What I want to focus on now is that when we asked ourselves *those* sorts of questions, we didn't find answers that pointed toward more schooling or to different schooling. Instead, we found out that our questions were rooted in fears that we couldn't honestly say would be resolved by school. We had no clear ideas of how learning would consistently happen outside of forced schooling, but we had the tools we needed to withdraw them from school as a start. What we had were two daughters who were not being listened to, not by their school and not by us. Adults were listening, but not in the ways that considered what we were hearing. Instead, we registered their fears as normal opposition that was our adult responsibility to help them work through, so they could stop being afraid and start being even better at schooling. And when they were labeled as Gifted and Talented, that surely affected our listening ears as well. We were listening to the fears of what could happen to them—how we could sabotage their proven, documented, impressive smartness if we didn't control their learning while they were young. Still, we were confronted with the reality of two girls relentless in their advocacy of themselves.

"I just have so many things to think about in my brain, but I don't have enough time to think about all my thoughts!" I can still see Marley's little elbows and fingers tracing the air around her while she expressed her feelings of frustration in kindergarten. We heard her words, but we honored our filters and fears over what she and, later, Sage, in very different ways, were telling us about why school wasn't working for them. Kris and I were extensions of the school system, and though Marley and Sage had plenty of caring adults around them, they had no allies willing to respect and trust what they were saying. And if they were in school all day, and then came home to allies of the school, who was actually listening to them? These were our questions that came before the questions about socialization or learning:

- If people constantly told them to keep doing something, despite their continued feelings against that thing, how could they grow up trusting and honoring their own feelings?

- Who could they trust to take a chance on them and show them that their feelings were relevant and valid?
- Did that sort of respect for people's (expressed) needs start when childhood ended?
- If we continued to pacify and disregard their assertions, were we trustworthy?

We weren't sure at all, but we suspected that it was worth exploring options outside of what they were experiencing, options that didn't find us choosing between our daughters' feelings and expressed needs and an institution's ideas about what our daughters needed.

Marley and Sage still haven't returned to school from that summer break in 2012. We took that chance, followed our daughters' requests for more time to do what they wanted to do. Our daughters' demands and pleas brought us to our family's first experience with crisis schooling, though we did not call it by that name. It took that one summer to find out that Marley and Sage were deep in crisis, they were drowning. Our experimental summer turned out to be a rescue mission, and we ended up rescuing ourselves from a way of life and a personal politic that was in direct opposition to the things we believed in. This singular focus on the best way to educate our daughters billowed out into liberation work, a practice of acknowledging and pivoting away from oppressive, control-centered relationships among people of any age over to something that centered consent, community, and lifelong learning. This is how we went from having "school-aged" children to raising free people. This is how we center learning, leadership, and liberation.

CHAPTER TWO

Using Mad Question-Askin' to Finally Start Changing Your Parenting Approach

"Marley, listen to me, you will bring your textbook to the beach, and it will be fun!"

I was trying to get this then nine-year-old to recognize how amazing it was that she could study and learn while laying mere feet from sea waters so clear and captivating. She wasn't buying my fake-ass enthusiasm. I was determined to stick to my story.

"But. I. Don't. Waaaant. To bring my book, Mama."

Her voice was low and steady, her big brown eyes firmly affixed on mine. She was used to textbooks and studying, and even enjoyed our trips to Barnes and Noble to get workbooks and pastries from the cafe inside the store, but now that we were in Jamaica, she was insistent that she would study at home not at the beach, because the beach was solely and non-negotiably for play. Kris and I had this exchange with that kid maybe three times in the first few weeks after we arrived on the island for our first extended trip. She and our then six-year-old, Sage, were on summer break, and we planned for six months on the island, with the hopes that this might transition into a long-term thing. We had enrolled them in a virtual academy that had a physical base in the US (Georgia), where we were based at the time. At my request, my mother shipped us the heavy-ass box of textbooks, and all the pockets of our checked baggage were already brimming with workbooks our daughters could use in between semesters at the virtual academy. We had our *responsible parents'* plan in place, but our experiences spending our days with Marley and Sage would alter those plans in ways neither Kris nor I could have ever freakin' imagined.

"Marley, you get to be *here* not in school, which is so good, right?"

"Yes, it is." She always held her chin a little higher when she suspected I was trying to run game on her. I was.

"And now you get to learn from books at home just like you wanted, right?"

"Yeah, Mama, but. . ."

"Listen to me, no buts, Marley!" I had to put my foot down and pull out my Oh, Babygirl, You Gon' Do What I Say Do card.

"You will bring and use your book, because you still have to learn."

That was our regular exchange, and it had gotten to the point that Marley wasn't even whiney or worked up with her resistance, she was just firm. She didn't throw tantrums; she was just hella insistent that she was not cool with bringing textbooks with her when we left home. The problem was that we left home a lot. Jamaica is a place that always has *something* going on. A simple taxi ride to the beach might end up being a four-hour experience chatting and laughing with strangers, being invited to eat another fish or drink another cup of something good or to some other activity, which made it hard to just leave home, run an errand, and come back. That's exactly why she needed to bring her textbook! The way I saw it, she'd never get any studying in if she didn't bring it with her. And then she'd be the B-word: Behind.

Of course, the exchanges always ended in her shouldering her bubblegum pink and cotton candy blue Dora the Explorer backpack filled with snacks, a sand shovel or two, and her textbook. She also shouldered me, lording over her, attempting to make sure she was covering whatever sections the academy had assigned for that week. Sage, being younger, had workbooks too, and she often resisted with a whiney "But whyyy?" but it was easier to keep her caught up with grade one and grade two work, so we didn't see her pushback as being as potentially detrimental to her learning as Marley's.

"I don't even care if I'm behind, Mama."

Marley was responding to my failed attempt at explaining how horrible it would be if not doing her textbook work caused her to fall behind. The skies were three shades of blue and a kiss of yellow, and the Caribbean Sea was on her usual sweet-singing flow. I wanted nothing more than to open a cold Red Stripe and sop up my fried snapper with the bammy and other savory goodness the seaside chef had heaped onto my piece of foil paper turned food tray. I was frustrated and losing my grasp on that feeling that I should talk to my children like people I loved and appreciated not mere subjects in my queendom. My response was always to get sterner and less listening-centered, especially because she and her sister had been deemed Gifted and Talented by their school, and I certainly didn't want to end up "messing up their Giftedness" from lack of them studying the right things. Honestly, the fact that Marley and Sage were viewed as particularly smart was one of the reasons I was afraid to listen to, let alone honor, their ongoing pleas to learn at home. So much of our perception of our daughters was rooted in what the school told us about them. If the tests said they were exceptional, then it was Kris's and my job to make sure they stayed that way, which meant we'd need to make sure we—the non-professional educators—didn't ruin that by doing anything crazy like listening to our daughters when they said they didn't want to study. Ironically, it was the Gifted and Talented label, or the school's practices toward children they'd given these labels, that prompted us to start paying more attention to our daughters' needs. I now scoff at those labels and see them as often (though, perhaps, not always) damaging and limiting, if not complete bullshit.

To back up a bit, toward the end of kindergarten the school asked our permission to test Marley for Giftedness.

Of course, this was exciting to Kris and me, and I personally felt like my efforts in my girls' earlier years with reading and writing were now showing up. It was about Marley, but, when I look back, it was also very much about me. I didn't recognize that back then, but now I can see clearly that the adult gaze—which we'll talk more about, for sure—was part of what was blocking our ears from listening to our daughters. Anyway, testing happened, labels were affirmed, and the school, with our permission and excitement, set out to figure out a way to meet Marley where she was intellectually. This is when the first set of alarm bells started going off. We said yes to that set of tests, but it turns out they were giving Marley more tests than we agreed to; testing her in blocks of time without our knowledge, let alone our permission.

One day Marley came home crying, because she had missed recess again, and that's how we found out she was being tested outside the times to which we'd consented.

Her missing recess mattered deeply to her and to us but not to her school. I made sure not to wear earrings that day. If you don't know the implications of that decision, ask Black women until you find one that can tell you with confidence. Anyway, we met with the offending parties the next day, and told them it had to stop. They agreed, complied, and then began the work of scheduling meetings with us and the school's Gifted teachers, as well as the school psychologist. I remember being in one group meeting and feeling very much like Kris and I were suspected of shady shit. By shady, I mean overworking her at home, making her study more than was healthy for a young child. People in the meeting were making statements like: "Kids need to be able to just play and be, not study all the time." She wasn't studying all the time. She did workbooks for about thirty minutes on the days she didn't have homework, as well as whenever she wanted to do workbooks. She enjoyed doing math workbooks with Kris, and the other workbooks were usually puzzles or sticker books with topics she chose during our bookstore runs. It seemed to us that it wasn't fathomable that Marley enjoyed academics, instead it must have been us forcing her to do these things, and, therefore, it must have stood to reason that she'd score so well on whatever battery of tests they ran.

Though the school did some things we did not like, we loved the teachers. Marley and Sage's teachers were wonderful women who clearly loved the work they did. Marley's kindergarten teacher had asked us if we had other children and actively vied to get Sage in her class when she realized we did, in fact, have another child who was going to start school soon. Mrs. B. looked out for our daughters and loved on them in ways that helped Kris and me feel comfortable that Marley's, and then Sage's, opposition to school had nothing to do with how they felt about their teachers or how their teachers felt about them. Fortunately, in our case, that love and care continued in varying ways with the various teachers with whom our girls engaged. One teacher said Marley was the type of child who reminded her why she got into teaching. Another teacher said if all her students were like Sage, she might not want to go home in the evenings, because she'd want to spend all her time being with them. What happened in school for Marley and Sage was not about their teachers, it was about the inherently damaging nature of forced, standardized curricula and a focus on studenthood over personhood. Their teachers, as engaged and caring as most of them were, had little more power than Marley and Sage—or Kris and me—over the structure of schooling and what it requires. As much as they saw Marley and Sage as children, school saw them as assets to develop, and that development called for choosing academics over personal needs and assertions. Every. Single. Time.

One example of this is the school's recommendation, after Marley's extensive testing bout, followed by trial runs in second, third, and fourth grade classes, to move Marley from the second-grade Gifted class (after being in first grade for a couple of months) into the fourth grade, with no regard for the emotional and social aspects of sitting in a room full of older children and being the only eight-almost-nine-year-old in the room. Out in the actual world, people who are a year or two apart in age aren't usually much different. In schooled settings, especially at the elementary/primary level, children in higher grade levels see themselves as vastly different from their younger, lower-grade-level student peers. Studenthood separates them, and Marley would need time to navigate that transition. The school didn't factor that in at all though, and the sounding alarm here was that the focus was clearly, unapologetically on academics not on the little girl involved in all of it. In school, reaching for the heights of studenthood was far more important than personhood and emotional wellness. It was at that point that Kris and I began having conversations about it being our job to support and nurture personhood and emotional wellness. Perhaps even more importantly, we began to see pinholes in the notion that personhood and emotional wellness could be nurtured within the requirements of conventionally structured education.

This is when Kris and I began asking the school fewer questions and started asking each other more questions. Notorious B.I.G.'s famous line about mad question-askin' became part of our regular mental soundtrack. I still use the term today, because, for us, it became a life skill and a lifeline back to our daughters and away from what their schooling was costing them. I define mad question-askin' (MQAs, if you're feelin' extra fly) as a process of questioning the intention behind your concern, instead of questioning to try to resolve your concern. MQAs seek out causes; regular questions focus solely on addressing symptoms. Can the school help us raise a whole person, or can they only help us gauge what she can handle academically? Should we be so focused on how much she can handle academically? And while we're addressing questions: Why was Marley saying that she didn't like school anymore, and that she wanted to stay at home, do her workbooks, go the bookstore, and watch *Fetch! with Ruff Ruffman*, the television series she called "her favorite learning program"?

Those questions arose, and we talked through them, but, at that time, Kris and I had become versed at being extensions of the school system, trusting its opinions and goals for our daughter above all. It's not as if we and the school put our heads together and decided what we wanted for her. No, the school said she was above and beyond and, therefore, could handle certain classes and environments, and we said, "Okay, let's see how we can implement this." We were operating as arms of the school system instead of being Marley's support system. We had deified the school system; it was our True North. This shitty realization—that we were operating like effective extensions of the school's ideas for Marley—brought to light for us just how much we had been ignoring or silencing *her* assertions in favor of the school's recommendations. She was asking about staying at home and learning at home, while we were beginning to see the chasm of a gap between what we wanted her to experience (feeling supported, heard, challenged by people who wanted the best for her) and what she was actually experiencing (feeling silenced, pushed, frustrated, and treated like some exciting result in the making). Marley began upping her requests to stay at home and learn from her "programs" (the TV shows she loved) and her workbooks. I was working primarily from home by then, but I was totally not about that at home teacher life. I had taught them how to read and how to write their names before they were four years old, and that's where I felt the depths of my teacher expertise ended. In discussing it over and over, it was clear neither Kris nor I were interested in enforcing a curriculum or checking work every day, and I felt really guilty about that truth. I also felt sure that as savvy and as educated as Kris and I were, we couldn't possibly know enough to teach our daughters at home, especially because we were not at all motivated to do so. We *wanted* to want to, but we just didn't.

We continued to look at ways to be more involved in the school system—joining the PTA Board, volunteering at the school more often—to offset its focus on academics over personhood. The more involved we became, the more we saw that we couldn't honor two directions at the same time. When Sage's time for school came along, her teacher said she saw similar signs of Giftedness, asked permission to give her the same tests Marley had gotten, assigned her the same labels, engaged the same push toward academics, all while her quiet, likes-to-be-alone personality amplified the school's lack of ability to honor a person's innate needs, while helping them to learn in ways that felt encouraging and engaging to them. Sage would often talk about how the children and teachers would "people on her" and how she liked her teacher but was bored with the classroom. She was frustrated with the noise and busyness and told us repeatedly that the time she spent at school *every single day* was, in her words, "way too forever long."

She wanted more time alone to do what she enjoyed. We couldn't see how that could hurt her, especially because she was vocal and curious out loud and loved books and relished using mixed materials to create "robots" and concepting "machines" that performed specific tasks that she was happy to explain in great, and I do mean great, detail, every time. She and I often shot videos where she'd explain her current project, robot, machine, or interest, in long-ass . . . er, I mean *great* detail, some of which I still have on my old YouTube channel. She was engaged in so many aspects of her environment and her own thoughts, but, back then, we didn't see that as enough. Still, even though we were still praying to the school gods, a new pattern was emerging. Our questions about our daughters' education were veering away from schooling and toward our children. Our concerns were more and more about our daughters as their own people and less and less about our daughters in relation to studenthood. We started looking at the pros and cons of our girls' educational path in its current form, and it became increasingly less feasible to ignore the ways the cons were towering over our perceived pros. For example, Marley, our social butterfly, loved being around other people, and everyone from the school nurse to the woman at the front desk knew Marley by name. She made it a point to visit them a few times per week on her way to wherever, to tell them they were each doing a good job. I know this because they all told me or Kris so, and since he and I were at the school all the damn time, sometimes at the same time, they had plenty opportunities to share these things with us. School for Marley, though filled with opportunities to meet her voracious appetite for *peopling*, was a constant source of frustration. She experienced what she repeatedly termed not having enough time to think her thoughts. She would talk about having watched an episode of *Fetch! with Ruff Ruffman* but not having enough time to think about all the parts of it. She loved to dissect whatever kept her interest, and she kept demanding time to do more of that. She loved to write out her thoughts, to draw characters that thought her thoughts, and to read stories about people and their experiences.

The more Kris and I talked and thought about our daughters' learning experiences, the more we realized that school actually wasn't the source of all their learning. This helped make it easier for us to listen to Marley and Sage's ongoing complaints about school, and we began to take their grievances seriously. We began to worry that dismissing their opinions about their learning might cause them to not trust themselves and their feelings. We weren't sure whether or not this was a bad thing—because maybe they shouldn't trust themselves, you know, being children and all—but it felt like something to keep paying attention to, so we did. And the more we paid attention to our daughters, the more cons we identified:

- Marley was losing her confidence. She got iffy about asking questions, often telling us she was worried about asking the wrong question or being too tired to ask any questions at all.
- Sage shifted from being comfortably introverted to painfully shy. She had always been quiet in most public spaces,

but at home she was vibrant and inquisitive. After her time in school, that began to change. She seemed to get frightened more easily, even by slight noises. She seemed more sensitive to sound and light. She constantly complained about being *peopled on*, never adjusting to the rhythm of standing in line with her finger over her lip like a *good* student. I tried going to the school less, because I thought maybe my presence there was making it harder for her to adjust; it didn't change anything. She said school made her sad.

These definitive statements from Marley and Sage kept coming, and so did the encouragement from their school for us to do what we could to keep our daughters on this brilliant track to stellar studenthood—that same track Kris and I started out feeling sure was the best thing for our daughters. But if it was so good for them, why were they so resistant? We couldn't keep ignoring those conflicting messages, and that's when and why we decided we'd use the summer break to feel through something, hell, anything, different than the conventional education path we had chosen for our daughters.

Before that summer ended, we withdrew them from school, reminding ourselves that if things didn't work out, we could always reenroll them. I began researching alternatives to conventional elementary school, found that virtual academy I told you about earlier, and decided that their fourth and first grade years would be their last in school, at least for a while. And, yes, even with all the questions we had, we still said yes to Marley moving to the fourth grade. Sage spent most of her first year and half of elementary school going between first and second grade classes, while; Kris and I spent most of our time trying to figure out how to make sure the girls stayed "ahead" but not to the detriment of the whole-person needs they each had and had expressed to us.

The virtual academy we settled on felt like a good start, because it still had a K-12 curriculum, but the girls could integrate their studies with engaging, time-ignoring activities that centered their own curiosities—and, of course, fun. We were still school-centered, just less so than before the girls started school. I say this because though the process to decide to withdraw took months and brought to light the ways our daughters' educational journeys were not healthy for them emotionally, we still essentially went from one master to another when we enrolled our daughters in a state virtual academy that followed the exact same K-12 standards as the school from which we'd freed them.

Fortunately, our willingness to try something different brought new resources and realizations to the fore—as is the case in many aspects of life. Along with the months of research and questioning we were doing, another molasses-slow process was being unearthed—the confines and heavy costs of lifestyle upkeep. A mortgage, a car payment, insurance for two vehicles, YMCA memberships, karate classes, gas prices, and the million little things in between. Kris and I had always loved to travel but had resigned ourselves to believing that it was only possible in short, expensive spurts, because children, because school, because money. However, after realizing that so much of our lives was confined to the school calendar and realizing we were, for the time being, free from that, we began exploring inexpensive travel options. We were both fully self-employed by then, and our projects just about covered our expenses and, more excitingly, didn't call for us to be in a particular location.

We were web-based in terms of our careers, which meant we could reimagine our lives and our locations. We set out to find the least expensive means to spend about a month somewhere besides Georgia, to simply see how that felt. We were fortunate to have cousins back home (Jamaica) who would rent us a small room inside their home. We couldn't rent that space and pay our mortgage though, so we decided we'd let our mortgage be late and just catch up as soon as we could. We needed to test this thing out—this way of living that allowed for virtual studies for Marley and Sage and the benefits of Kris and me already being based online in terms of serving our clients. We never needed to meet anyone in person, him being a creative branding specialist and graphic designer, and me being a freelance writer and emotional wellness coach. So with the fear-facing and risk-taking—we found tickets to Jamaica within our measly budget, finalized our housing arrangements in Kingston, and went for it. That's how we ended up in that ongoing argument about beautiful beaches and necessary textbooks.

"Fine, Marley." I hadn't the energy or the desire to continue what had become our weekly unwanted ritual. "You know what? Don't learn anything then. We'll take some time off, so you girls can get a break, and then you'll come back to this without a single word besides 'Yes, Mama,' you hear me?"

Her little eyebrows were all furrowed, and her bottom lip was starting to quiver. She was looking out past me at the water and didn't even seem relieved. Perhaps, like me, she was tired of our regular exchange.

"Oh. Kay." she replied flatly. I told myself I'd explain to Kris what happened, and then in a few weeks we'd get back on track. Sage wasn't as resistant as Marley, but as she was also younger, we felt less afraid about her not learning what she *needed* to be learning. We felt more comfortable with her doing some workbooks a few times a week, accented by conversations and activities meant to ensure she was always learning something. When I talked to Kris, he was fine with the new plan, and, as it turns out, our new plan paved the way for something completely unplanned, a way of living and learning together that felt natural and exciting, scary at times, but that was always showing us how little we knew about learning and how much we'd been conflating learning with schooling. That was 2012, and as that year progressed we never did get back to that original plan. Instead, we developed into skilled observers, witnessing the vast and varied ways that Marley and Sage learned about a variety of things without input from

Kris, me, or textbooks. We began to see that a big part of our job at that time was to become better at witnessing the ways that learning was already happening, instead of worrying about pushing what we had seen as learning, based on what was required in school or in the many workbooks and other materials based on the standard K-12 curriculum.

Years later, in 2017, in my constant efforts to find other freedom-minded families with children, I came to learn that another family was having a very similar experience, though under very different circumstances. A Virginia-based, multi-hyphenate creative named Yolonda Coles Jones (who I met on Instagram) and her husband Will, who, at the time of writing, are full-time entrepreneurs raising two girls and twin boys. Their family's shift to unschooling is a prime example of how life and perspective changes when we start to understand how learning happens. Yolonda and Will started out with their daughters in a conservative Christian Homeschooling environment. That's all they'd seen around them, and so Yolonda (the primary at-home parent during that time) only saw noninstitutional education through that particular homeschooling lens.

After evolving their own personal beliefs and watching how the (book) lessons and (social) experiences didn't feel relevant to their children, they took a step back to first figure out what was happening, and then how to reconfigure it to fit their girls' interests and needs. Yolonda started researching educational alternatives, but a surprise pregnancy caused those plans to get tossed out the window, especially since the real surprise was that they were having twin boys! Life's pace sped up for their family after that. Wanting to prepare for the financial shift that would come with two more children, they moved in with family to save and to plan for their future. They also upped their entrepreneurial efforts, but Yolonda's boys needed her to be still. Her doctor put her on bedrest for almost her entire pregnancy. Yolonda was frustrated at first but came to call that time at home her "cosmic revelatory place." She sat up in bed each day, watching her daughters learn, while feeling bad about not being able to educate them the way she knew.

"As I was growing my sons," she told me when I interviewed her in 2017 for my unschooling podcast, "I was watching my daughters develop their own interests in certain books, certain types of toys, certain things on television," she marveled. "I was forced to sit still and watch them, and from that space I began to understand and really be astonished . . . they are learning on their own! They are acquiring language, navigating difficult circumstances. In conversation and in the living, look at how much they're learning! So when the boys were born, in came all these other logistics of having twin babies. We all had to learn to be flexible, and then I came into consciousness about mindfully engaging with our children, engaging in their interests through real-life happenings— asking questions at doctor's visits and so many opportunities for learning outside the windows of Monday through Friday."

At the time we spoke, Yolonda's daughters were doing a fusion of studies that helped them dive further into their interests. Among their four children, Will and Yolonda are raising science geeks, some serious multi-instrument musicians, and voracious readers, not to mention that they now produce books and online resources to show the results of trusting children and understanding learning without the limitations of schooling. Among self-directed communities, Yolonda and Will's story is commonplace, and their brilliant children, Kris and I would eventually learn, are not anomalies. It turns out that this is how humans evolve when they are in supportive learning environments with people who trust them, and who have educated themselves about the biology and psychology of human learning. This way, self-directed-ness, isn't some preferred learning method, it's evidence of how learning happens.

Like Yolonda and Will, Kris's and my growing witnessing skills fully rerouted our ideas about how children gained knowledge and applied it. Sometimes it was subtle, like having a conversation with Sage about something happening in the news, for example, and realizing that she was making connections and using words we didn't know she knew. Other times, it was jaw-dropping, like the number of books the girls would read on my Kindle without being prompted and the conversations, art, and requests for particular activities that would come out of their reading. We began to slowly shift our thoughts from textbooks and virtual academies to becoming better witnesses, and it was then that we began to see our daughters as natural learners instead of good fourth and first graders.

CHAPTER THREE

How Freedom from Schooling Made Room for Affordable, Extensive Travel (and Brand-New Parenting Fears)

During that first year of life without a focus on going into a physical school, we spent our time happily snacking and sweating into our days. We didn't have planned lessons or teaching moments. We said yes to invitations to day-long road trips to neighboring parishes. One festival took us nearly two hundred kilometers (approximately 125 miles) from Montego Bay to a town named Hope Bay, just north of Port Antonio, the capital city of what is arguably Jamaica's most beautiful parish, Portland. For about three and a half hours, we sang, told and relished stories, and shared our excitement about food and drums and performances by renowned musicians, dancers, and folklorists. This particular outdoor festival celebrated the island's African heritage, including our ancestors—it was called *Fi Wi Sinting*. The name basically means *Our Thing* and comes with a sense of pride in ownership; this is our thing, and we're proud of that! We spent the whole day in Port Antonio, getting home near midnight, after leaving that morning before sunrise. This was not an exceptionally unique day for us. Our new normal included spontaneous awesomes, like all-day trips to different beaches, marveling at the rich colors of the land and the birds during nature hikes, creating hand-drawn maps of our new neighborhoods, watching TV shows (ones that we considered back then to be "educational" content), and lots of meeting new people and spending time chatting with them about where they were visiting from or where they lived, if they were local, and all the interesting things that can come from organic conversation.

Though we left lots of space for Marley's and Sage's interests and for free time, we were not unschooling yet, but we were clearing the way for unschooling to happen eventually. We (Kris and I) were using training wheels, and the learning process was slow and not exactly steady. I would have repeated moments of panic, where I'd be so sure that Marley and Sage were being shortchanged and that I should probably get more serious about their learning. By more serious, I basically meant more forceful. On the days when the girls seemed engaged in things outside the house, I was fine. But if they watched one too many cartoons, or if they failed one of my verbal pop quizzes on math, history, or geography (which I did all the time), I'd tell myself the story that I was failing them, and that the only way to fix that was for Kris and me to do more things for the girls, which basically meant assigning them more things to do. Each time I acted on that fear, I'd get a response that told me that my reaction was just that, a fear-based trigger reaction not a response that I had felt through and assessed based on what I was observing with Marley and Sage.

My observation was that they were picking up things (ideas, clarity, new curiosities) that we weren't directly offering them. They didn't need to be taught all the time; they learned a lot of things without ever being taught those things or having those things offered as something educational for them to do. For example, we took them to a cultural festival to learn more about the history of Jamaica, but Sage became temporarily obsessed with a particular fruit we saw. Neither she nor I can remember what fruit it was, but I know she wanted to know everything there was to know about that fruit. She'd want to eat it, cook it, freeze it, paint it, sketch it, learn where it came from, learn which birds or other animals ate it, what other colors it had throughout its growth process, everything about the fruit. We'd see that she and Marley studied things they were interested in, even when—actually, it's more like *especially* when—they chose that thing themselves. After about a month of observation, we packed up the virtual academy's books, knowing we'd send them back in pristine condition, because we probably would never crack them open again. We threw up peace signs to that notion of seeing textbooks as children's main access to layered historied information. We were still assigning our girls specific tasks that we thought would foster necessary learning. We were doing a lot of math and geography, especially local geography, because we felt that we couldn't trust them to practice that themselves, and if they didn't practice those skills, their lives would be somehow less than. As we'll get into later, that belief and need diminishes and eventually heals as you continue to unschool and inevitably meet unschooling's ever-present companion, deschooling. What that six-week stint in Jamaica did for us, though, was whet our collective appetites for living together and help us start to see how childhood learning is a by-product of living in community with adults who have the time and space to prioritize deep exploration of whatever interests children have.

We began in the summer of 2012, and by November of the following year, we'd reconfigured our lives to do our first six-month stay on the island, this time in Montego Bay, enjoying its slower (than Kingston) pace, cheaper housing and locally grown produce, old mansions and factories that offered cheap or free tours, and even easier access to amazing beach towns and fishing villages full of friendly people who want to sell you the best seafood and tell you the most hilarious stories. One particular fishing village named Fisherman's Beach and one of its charismatic residents, a Rasta man called Sleepy, became major sources of wonderful socializing and vast, deep learning for the four of us. Marley and Sage spent hours on the water, in boats with the children who lived at Fisherman's Beach, while Kris and I talked to whoever was present about whatever was top of mind for them or us, easy, emergent conversation that ended up being cyphers of cultural exchange and deepening. We learned the history behind that particular village. Sleepy walked us across the street to introduce us to farmers and other vendors of the local market. They gave us great deals on every kind of fresh, local produce imaginable, asked us what fruits and veggies they should bring us from the country, and always had an extra mango or some oranges or soursop to gift to Marley and Sage. We watched our daughters become increasingly comfortable talking with adults and converting Jamaican dollars to US dollars to make sure they were giving and getting the right monies when we shopped. It was so good to be in everyone's company, and we all learned so much more than we could have in any classroom.

By this point, Kris and I had begun to glimpse the early era of what would become our unschooling practice. We were still pretty schoolish, so the shift that was happening wasn't really a shift in me or Kris at all. What happened is that our idea of learning began to shift, as we realized that learning was not a thing that happened from a teacher or guide or parent to a child or student. Instead, learning is multidirectional and multidimensional. I was certainly learning a lot through Marley and Sage—that's one direction. Another is that they were now experimenting with me and Kris, learning to trust us not only to lead but to listen. They experimented through things like calling on us to walk our talk about them being free to show their true feelings, because they had them, just like we did. They were experimenting with trusting us not only to solve things for them but, more importantly, to sit with them while they learn to trust themselves to solve things without us. Learning wasn't this top-down thing; it came from various directions, and, for the first time, we were beginning to glimpse them. I also see learning as multidimensional, because we saw it coming from books and learned people, but it also came from silence, from cartoons, from birds and plants and seashells, and from shit we couldn't explain but could feel and deeply appreciate. What shifted was that we were becoming educated by Marley's and Sage's words, their actions, and their moments of silence. We were beginning to realize how uneducated we were, and it caused what I think is the highest form of currency in this Raising Free People practice: curiosity.

We really stretched our curiosity muscles when we stopped thinking that keeping our house in Georgia was the thing worth fighting for. We realized that we now had access to the vast world of airline ticket prices and apartment rentals during the low seasons. We were no longer confined to traveling during school breaks, when all the flights and accommodations were most expensive. We also no longer needed to live in that particular neighborhood, because our daily design was no longer centered on proximity to that school (or any, for that matter). So, slowly, instead of focusing on how to make more money to cover our mortgage and expenses and travel in between paying for our life, we became curious about becoming location independent. We became curious about whether or not the house still met the needs and priorities we now had. We bought that house, the second piece of real estate we'd bought together, specifically because of the school district it was in. Now that school districts didn't mean much to us, we began to shift our energies, including our money, toward where our priorities were—spending more time with our daughters, familiarizing ourselves with the ways learning happened outside of schooling, living cheaper, finding opportunities to explore new-to-us parts of Jamaica together, and making that lifestyle financially sustainable. While we were living in that space and sorting through it all, we had definitely begun deschooling, particularly around the ideas of children, money, and respect.

What is Deschooling?

Quoting Wikipedia ain't the best practice, but the word is not in the dictionary, so I'll use it here just for context:

Deschooling is the mental transition a person goes through after being removed from a formal schooling environment. It usually refers to children who have been removed from school for the purpose of unschooling. But technically the term applies to any person leaving school, either by dropping out or graduating.

Sure, that's the origin of the word in the context of education, but, more than that, deschooling is the shift that happens after mad question-askin' starts working. Here's my two-part definition of deschooling:

- shedding the programming and habits that resulted from other people's agency over your time, body, thoughts, or actions;
- designing and practicing beliefs that align with your desire to thrive, be happy, and succeed.

Deschoolers (a name for people who see themselves as actively involved in deschooling) who are deep in the work begin to see and understand the ways various types of oppression (often perpetuated through school's focus on standardizing learning), if left undisrupted, intersect and strengthen each other, causing painful relationship dynamics between us and people we love. The questions that led us to liberate our daughters from forced schooling, now, nearly two years into our journey, had led us to a different, related set of "aha" moments. It broadened our focus from just learning to the whole ecology of living together. It was no longer just about our approach to learning but our approach to parenting overall. Just as we'd shifted from trying to figure out how to get Marley and Sage to settle into stellar studenthood to looking at a whole-person approach to learning, we now needed to look at how that whole person was being treated, not just how they were learning. One day, Marley wrote me a note that challenged me to look at this idea of living with a child in a way that demonstrated respect and regard not control and coercion, like we were doing by forcing them to go to school. The note read: "Please, I am not in the mood to talk, so don't talk to me unless I ask you something. This is no disrespect I hope. Thx, Marley."

Quick question: Do you know anything about Jamaican parents? Island parents, for that matter? This is absolutely a generalization here, but, dammit, it's a safe one, because most people raised by island people will quickly tell you: Island. Parents. Don't. Play. Respect, the way they define it, is non-negotiable, and the spectrum of things a child can do to disrespect an adult, especially a parent, is miles wide and deep. Reverence for adults, not just respect, is expected, normalized, and deeply ingrained. Somebody else's mama could slap you for not showing reverence to any adult. Physical punishment for the wrong displays of emotion, even silent ones like frowns or subtle ones like deep sighs, were commonplace, expected, celebrated as one of the reasons children "turned out right." Not only did you, as a child, dismiss any attitudes or anything adults might perceive as rudeness, your general countenance should reflect a constant respect—no space at all for showing actual emotion, if that emotion was contrary to what was reverent and pleasant for the adults in your life— again, especially your parents. So when Marley wrote me that note, a big part of my brain said, "Hell no! If giving her more space to explore and express herself means she's gonna be disrespectful at nine years old, this shit is over. Oh. Ver."

But that thought was fleeting. The thoughts that stayed, the ones that I pondered and talked with Kris about repeatedly, raised versions of one pressing question: Is this more respectful way of living with children gonna end up with us raising self-centered snobs who focus primarily on what they feel and need, with little regard for cultural values like respecting adults up in here?

In other words, will they be expressive and emotionally well or just *bright an' facety* (a Jamaican patois term that essentially means disrespectful and without apology)? These were questions I didn't remember having when the girls were in school. They were practiced in the art of genuflecting, both because of our environment at home and, of course, because of the structure of schooling—children knew *their place*. But I knew that never sat well with me, if only to some extent. Now, while I was experiencing that note as potentially bright an' facety, it felt like allowing our daughters their right to express themselves and other practices centered on raising a healthy whole person was taking this risky, respect-based parenting thing too far! Again, mad question-askin' was part of our process: Shouldn't she feel afraid to talk to (or write to) me like that? Wasn't that something I should address before she was straight up cursing me out and calling me a bitch like my first American friend Sophia did to her mom?

I witnessed Sophia call her mom a bitch and slam her room door the very first year I moved to America. When I told my mother about it, she sucked her teeth, glared at me, and spoke like she held me somehow complicit. Mom spoke in a stern, sharp tone, warning me against taking on those behaviors and losing my perfectly good teeth as a result. Okay, I'm exaggerating about what Mom said. I don't actually remember her words, but I damn sure remember the seriousness in her cautionary tone.

Fact is, she did not have to warn me, because prior to moving to America when I was ten years old, I was being raising by my loving, very traditional, religious grandmother in Jamaica, and all my interactions with adults up to that point reinforced the idea that I was not allowed to express any level of dissent, let alone direct profanity, out loud at any of them, and certainly not to one that was in charge of my body. In my mind, Marley was 2.2 seconds away from being Sophia, and I needed to gather all my island parenting and hurl it at her, lest she get it twisted. But, again, that thought was fleeting; it wasn't rooted in my actual truth about parenting. And that truth ran contrary to how I was raised and how all the young people I knew (except, of course, Sophia) were raised.

My truth was that I was raising a little girl who would grow up to be a Black woman in a country that routinely silences Black women. I knew it wouldn't be the best thing for me to focus on how my daughter's feelings made me feel. My reaction to her truth couldn't be the most important aspect of her expressing her truth. But the other truth in the room was that the way Marley wrote the note to Kris and me raised some emotions, fears, and insecurities that were now front and center. Her honest self-expression felt like backlash from allowing her to be honest out loud to us, her parents. This is probably one of the first times I began to recognize a direct connection between my work as a parent and my beliefs around issues of social justice. Was I willing to silence a Black woman-becoming because I didn't like how her words made me feel? When Kris and I talked about it, questions came flooding in again, and they were in the realm of:

- Were we willing to give up our power in exchange for our daughters' freedom?
- Did we have to? Is that how this thing worked?
- Wouldn't it be easier, and isn't it a necessary boundary, for us to be able to dart either of our daughters a look that would have them instantly reconsider doing or saying anything that would make us, their respect-deserving parents, feel uncomfortable or, worse yet, disrespected?
- Was it actually disrespectful to have feelings and to express them, especially in the way she had?

Further we went into the shift from no more school to the exploration of raising a person free to express themself. Surely, there was a way to express one's self without being disrespectful. But that wasn't the real question; the real question was: Why was I viewing this as disrespectful? I realized that I wasn't. I was, however, very aware of the fact that other adults around me might see it that way, and that's what I was reacting to in that moment. It wasn't about Marley's note; it was about the *adult gaze*. Marley was allowed to have emotions, but they couldn't make me look like I was raising a disrespectful child; that was my problem with it, and that was my issue to address and resolve, not my chance to make her do something other than express herself. If I forced her to suppress those feelings, I'd be replacing the former master of schooling with this new one of other adults' opinions about my daughter's feelings.

And what would it say to her if I centered other people's concerns around politeness and self-expression above her feeling safe enough with Kris and me to ask for and expect to get space to process her feelings? Wasn't that a life skill I was still working on? Wasn't this a good thing?

All the right questions were coming up, and, again, not many "ahas" or answers. Mostly, my questions led me back to my insecurities, along with my recognition of all the things that influence our relationships with our children, including our (in this case, *my*) concern around how I might be perceived as a parent who was not in control of her child. As we traveled and met new people often, there were plenty of chances to practice observing myself, my physical and emotional reactions to people's opinions (or, sometimes, *my perception* of people's opinions) about my children and, by proxy, my parenting. New fears were vying for the top of my long list of parenting woes. Learning was dropping lower on the list, because I saw that it happened even when we were deliberate about "not learning anything" or "just playing around." What was on the rise were a set of fears that had to do with my perception—and other adults' perceptions—of respect. More specifically:

- Could I raise children who were in charge of their own learning and their own time *and* were still motivated to be respectful?
- What the hell was respectful, anyway? Who decides that?
- Why did I need other adults to respect the way I parented? Was that about respect, or was that about approval?

- How much better would my relationships be if I knew, like Marley, how to ask for the space that I needed?

  Shit.

More questions with no "aha" moments. But, still, plenty of direction.

CHAPTER FOUR

The Shift in Power That Eventually Rooted Us in Unschooling

As my family continued our practice of living in more mindful relationships with each other over the next year and a half, I was compelled to process my experiences through writing. I have always used writing, and it has used me, to explore and express myself. Exploration was the main thing happening back then, and the self-exploration aspect proved far more layered than I could have ever imagined. I began to realize that unschooling and deschooling were personal processes that directly influenced our relationships with everything—not just children, not just school, not just learning. It was personal leadership work; it was shedding, sorting, and shifting one's way out of layers of expectations into authentic self-discovery. I wrote things down in my attempts to make sense of it all, and I was writing mainly about parenting and the shifts within it that Kris and I were experiencing. I published an online self-study course about it, hosted live workshops that centered it, and sat in community with other parents doing spontaneous, emotional, liberating cyphers around more deschooling-minded way of being with our children. It felt freeing to share and to finally begin finding community! And, for sure, the entire practice of being so curious and present with my children began to feel to me like the makings of a type of liberation from old norms that were not only great for Marley and Sage but liberating for Kris and for me. It felt so good to not be nearly as concerned about how other adults were experiencing our children, and when Marley killed the Easter Bunny, and the offended parent expressed their concerns with Marley's actions, our response informed me that we were, in fact, experiencing a transformation in how we parented. Before I tell you about the transformation, let me tell you about this bunny murder.

Before our lifestyle transition, we were raising our daughters in a suburb with the other picket fence–chasin' folks. One day, during a neighborhood women's gathering, one of our neighbors pulled me aside to talk to me about a concern she had. She began to explain her frustrations with how my daughter (this was back in about 2011, so Marley was about seven at the time) had upset the balance of something "holy" (I guess) by telling her son (Marley's classmate) that the Easter Bunny was not real. Homegirl was upset— Upsettt—and droned on about the lengths to which she and her husband had to go in attempts to repair whatever trauma my child had apparently caused their son. Real talk, I stopped listening after a short while. I found her concerns ridiculous— slow-blink, lip-curl, girl-bye! ridiculous. I believe that every family has the right to impart whatever beliefs and customs resonate with them. No other adult has the right to try to alter the beliefs of a child in ways that are contrary to what their parents choose to impart. But when it comes to other children's opinions, the reality is different. Had I, as an adult, made it my business to offer opposing perspectives to her son on bunnies that laid eggs and whatnot, *that* would have been out of line. But *I* did not; my daughter, her son's classmate and peer, did. And when I asked Marley about the context of the bunny conversation, I saw that she didn't say it maliciously but matter-of-factly, because she thought her classmate, let's call him Kevin, was joking, just as she'd be joking if she told someone that the Easter Bunny brought her things for Easter. Now, I know Kevin's mamma was upset at what Marley told her son, but I think she was even more upset that her telling me about my daughter's perceived transgression didn't result in what she'd hoped for—acquiescence. We were pre-unschooling back then, so I wasn't putting the situation through the same filters I would now, but we were living in a predominantly White neighborhood (we were one of three Black families in our entire complex) and had worked in predominantly White corporate environments, so I was and am really familiar with the energy and the expectation; I picked up what homegirl was laying down. What she was seeking from Marley, through me, was an apology. My child made her family uncomfortable by believing or acting in a way that is different than what her family does or believes, and it was our job to fix that discomfort, to fall in line. I was supposed to use my dominion over my child, make her apologize, and do my part to make Easter great again for our neighborhood. It wasn't gonna happen. Still ain't happened.

As a parent, I see that as an opportunity not an issue. Those instances create opportunities to dialogue around differences, respect for those differences, and, of course, the right and practice of expressing one's own beliefs without belittling the beliefs of others. We've had plenty of practice in this area, since one child told Marley that she was going to hell for not believing in Jesus, among other threats. Our neighbor seemed surprised that I did not offer her an apology and refused to "have a talk with my kid" about why what she did was wrong. Instead, I told her that we talk to our daughters about the fact that other families believe, and have a right to believe, in Santa Claus, the Easter Bunny, and other religious mascots, just as we have the right to believe something different. Still, our daughters do not shy away from conversations about religion or their opinions about those religious beliefs. Should I try to stop them from being willing to tackle tough topics? Naah, I don't think so. Ultimately, I told that concerned mama that my daughter was not in charge of their son's reality or the preservation of the reality his parents are working to create. Were we to hold any child, or even the school, to that same standard, there would be no holiday celebrations that focused on pilgrims, Jesus, Santa, the Easter Bunny, or some of the other subtler activities and lessons that, in my opinion, qualify as religious elitism.

Would you have spoken to your child about bursting the boy's Easter Bunny bubble? Did I miss an opportunity to raise a child more sensitive to other people's beliefs? Kris and I asked each other those questions and decided that we were comfortable with how the situation was handled. We weren't insensitive to homegirl's complaint, it just wasn't more important than Marley's beliefs, and her son's Easter Bunny was not going to take priority over Marley's whatever. They were classmates having a discussion, and Marley did not wield any power over her son, she simply gave her opinion. An opinion that will be overshadowed a million times over by all the marketing and narratives that will remind that woman's son that for many, many people, just like him, the Easter Bunny is a total (real?) thing. I, for sure, would've handled that differently a year prior. This was 2015, and by then I felt like Kris and I had broken open as a result of this new examining of the parenting choices he and I were making. We were ready to parent in ways that did not tell or show Marley and Sage that they were only allowed to exist or express themselves in ways that kept the adults around them comfortable. By this time, we had released all nonconsensual education and had a better (though not thorough) understanding of how to support Marley and Sage's natural learning process. By this time, we were unschooling.

What Is Unschooling?

Unschooling is a child-trusting, anti-oppressive, liberatory, love-centered approach to parenting and caregiving. It is a way of life that is based on freedom, respect, and autonomy.

Unschooling is a curiosity-led approach to learning without testing and predefined curricula. Unschoolers see learning as an organic by-product of living and being a child and, therefore, reject the premise of passing information from adults and books to children based on what is believed (by adults) to be necessary learning. Children follow their interests, and their parents offer resources, which can include direct instruction and books, for their children to pursue, exploring what they enjoy. Unschooling is a way of life that is based on freedom, respect, and autonomy. Listening and witnessing help parents to facilitate learning by offering resources for their child to pursue their interests and to follow their curiosity, without the restrictions of time limitations or judgment by way of testing.

Deschooling and unschooling are healing work as much as they are liberation-centered lifestyle practices. I recognized that my healing was necessary for me to parent using a lens of liberation. Respecting autonomy was central to unschooling now. It had far surpassed the focus on ways to replace school. It was now about *Power*. Having power over children was the norm, and it was abused, so this work was about switching to a more partnership-centered approach to parenting that allowed for the modeling and the practice of the same types of things I discussed and even wrestled with as a feminist. I remember writing a piece that year about how Sage's resistance to bras was the current core of my deschooling practice; in my diary, I called that period in our lives Bra Battle 2015. That set of experiences opened my eyes to my own issues with bodily autonomy and how those unresolved issues were playing out in my parenting. Bra Battle 2015 was yet another lesson in the reality that unschooling was not so much about what to learn or how to learn but, instead, about how to nurture trust and a child's sense of autonomy, while recognizing and unpacking your own colonized ideas about what it means to be in a body, especially as a woman, and even more particularly as a Black woman. Let me explain.

By the time Sage was nine years old, she had full breasts, but she refused to wear bras of any kind. She told me she didn't see the point of them. When I first introduced bras as something for her, she asked me if I wore my bra for medical reasons. I was surprised by the question, and my default response was: "Yes, because otherwise my breasts would hurt all the time." I don't even know why I said that. All I know is that I felt it was my responsibility to try to convince her that she needed to be wearing a bra. As is the pattern with Marley and Sage, they suss out parenting fears and call our asses out. Sage continued to ask me about my rationale for this bra-pushing I was doing, and I think she kept doing that because she suspected my words were rooted in fear. She was right; some of it was my pure ignorance around the purpose of bras and the anatomy of breasts, but much of it was also about fear—fear that her new breasts would invite unwanted attention and fear that she'd have long, saggy breasts by the time she was twenty-five, because her mother didn't reinforce *smart titty rules* or some shit. When I recognized that I was fear-focused, I changed my focus and got brave. Bravery in this instance looked like researching the medical need (or lack thereof) for bras, checking out blogs and books about body appreciation and confidence to see how other parents handled this, and being honest about my own misinformation on breasts and bras.

Did you know that there is no medical reason why girls or women should wear bras when they develop breasts? In fact, those old tales about long breasts being the result of bad bras or not sleeping in bras at night are just that—tales with no foundation in any biological or medical proof, probably perpetuated by our society's focus on the male gaze. Realizing that, I finally felt comfortable ending my (unsuccessful but persistent) bullying approach to bra-wearing. Instead, I told her about the research I'd done and the conclusions I had come to. She and I spent hours skimming articles about breasts and bras, nipple policing, and body positivity. We also talked about times when wearing a bra might be beneficial. I gave her examples of professional environments or exercising or just wanting a sleek look for a particular type of shirt or dress. I had successfully partnered with Sage, so that we could discover a solution together. Sage is thirteen as I write this, and not to get all up in her business, but she now opts for sports bras if she feels she wants support or coverage. More importantly, she understands why wearing a bra is about personal choice, and that she has the right to be part of the choices that have to do with her body. I can only imagine how much I would've missed in terms of trust-building, partnership, and relieving myself of my own ignorance had I chosen to stick to my stance and force Sage to wear a bra. After I got comfortable with her choice, I was able to feel even further into my own resistance to her decision. I could see, in hindsight, that this was another example of my parenting being rooted not just in fear but in the one of the other gazes. We've talked about the male gaze, but let's talk about the adult gaze too:

- What would people think if my daughter didn't wear a bra?
- What message would that send to boys about her?
- Shouldn't she conform to what was expected?
- Would her not wearing a bra make it easier for people to sexualize her body, and if something happened to her (sexual assault, for example) would it not, therefore, be tied to me not making sure she was doing the "right" thing and covering her breasts?

Mad question-askin' paved the way to powerful pauses and observations yet again. In this case, it took me down a road of extensive research, and the results were, once again, less about my daughter's resistance and more about the ways I needed to prioritize my ongoing deschooling process, so that I didn't use my position of power to participate in the sort of oppression of people that I claimed to be against in the world. I spent the year after that experience deep in research and personal inquiry around what I came to understand as bodily autonomy. Prior to that, I think I viewed my daughters' bodies as my property, just like the law does. As I unpacked my own unquestioned rules about bodies—mine, my daughters', and bodies in general—I began to see the tragic connection between my history as a Jamaican raised within the boundaries and fears of a loving yet religious family that, like many of the heavily religious families we knew back then, was also subject to colonizer-centered ideas about how we should manage ourselves, our bodies, our minds, and our actions. As a girl, it was my job to cover up my body so that wayward boys and men didn't want it. It was my job to present a body that was modest and socially acceptable in size and attire. The adults in charge of me were responsible for overseeing my body and telling me what to do with it, in accordance with the rules they had been taught to follow.

If I had said to my grandmother or my mother that I didn't want to wear a bra, and if I had the ovaries to stand my ground the way Sage did, I would have probably been hit, repeatedly, from a place of what my family would have seen as love, responsibility, and care. Through their lens, it would have been their job to make me do with my body whatever they saw fit, and I took that approach with Sage at first, until her assertions and resistance routed me in a different direction. In the years following that early conversation, Sage would teach me more about the ways that my approach to parenting was heavily tainted by the effects of colonization and how, as a parent, I walked the grounds of both colonizer and colonized, using the ways colonization had affected the adults who raised me to now attempt to raise my children. Hitting my children, seeing them as property in some ways, silencing their voices to the benefit of my own. Presenting them to the world in ways that made me and the world comfortable, without prioritizing how it made my children feel. This is when I began to realize that, as unschoolers, my children's resistance is often my roadmap, not only to parenting but also to my own decolonization efforts, my own liberation work.

Three Mistakes Parents Make When Teaching Consent and Bodily Autonomy—and How to Fix Them

About a year after Bra Battle 2015 and all the "aha" moments that would follow, I ended up writing and selling a nearly 2500-word essay on bodily autonomy and probably spent about 2500 hours assessing my and Kris's roles in how my daughters view and engage in bodily autonomy. The essay was also published as part of an anthology on consent. Here's that essay:

I often hear people talk about pregnancy from a space of gratitude—and sometimes excitement. Though I agree that the journey is incredible and enriching, there is another, perhaps less embraced aspect: for me, pregnancy was also full of moments of intense vulnerability, fear, and, at times, anger. I felt fearful about my own safety, it being so inextricably linked with the safety of the person growing in my belly.

Inadvertent pushes from someone who stood in a line behind me, an overly-ambitious driver who darted across me at an intersection, a woman who threatened me because she (wrongly) assumed I stole her parking spot—all those instances of intense vulnerability and primal fear stemming from my need to protect my future child. Even more unnerving were the instances where physical contact with my belly wasn't just implied, *it was accomplished*.

This is where my anger would rise to the surface—I'd get angry at the people who felt completely within their rights to touch my belly, to touch my baby. Whether an elderly man or a woman who was also a mother, I resented them for feeling okay with touching my child without permission, even when she was in utero.

For sure, I felt uncomfortable with them trying to touch *my* body—and all that that says about being a woman in public space.

But more than that, it clued me in to many adults' idea that they don't need children's permission to touch them—or to require that they touch someone else.

Today, my daughters are twelve and ten, and I still feel the need to protect them physically—and to advocate for their right to govern their own bodies. But I have to do more than advocate for them. In a world that constantly sends messages to women about connecting their value with their physicality and desirability, I need to help them operate with an awareness of their right to reject or accept physical touch or any act that affects their personal space or feeling of safety, from any adult or child.

And that means I have to be honest about the ways that I, myself, might infringe on their personal boundaries, and I have to facilitate these conversations with the adults around me. I don't just mean conversations about what we can do to protect children but about what we must do to help children understand their options for protecting their physical and emotional selves.

One way we can approach this goal is to explore some of the common mistakes we adults make when it comes to helping children practice bodily autonomy, which is at the root of consent culture for children. Otherwise, we will continue to do the things that compromise the self-confidence, the sense of safety/bodily autonomy, and the mental wellness of the children we love. Because the reality is that children are coerced into situations where their bodies are treated as the property of their parents. The instances vary from making them hug a family member to trading their body for sex, drugs, or even food. All of these instances can send a message to children that their bodies are not their own. They also blur the lines between safe and unsafe touch, or consent versus coercion, and make it difficult for many children to identify when they're being inappropriately or uncomfortably touched by an adult or another child.

Many of us send messages that lessen their ability to recognize and trust what feels safe and what feels uncomfortable for them, as well as how to confidently communicate with an adult that they trust when their personal boundaries are violated by anyone, including an adult or child they know and trust.

Statistically, the percentages are wildly unnerving: 90 percent of child sexual abuse victims know the perpetrator in some way, and 68 percent are abused by family members. What's more staggering is that 90 percent are abused by someone they know, love, or trust, and 20 percent of child sexual abuse victims are under the age of eight. Most of them don't tell until they become adults. One of the reasons for this is that as children they didn't have language around those feelings. No one was talking to them about their right to feel safe in their own bodies—to have and assert personal boundaries as a way of protecting themselves.

Consent culture is often confined to the topic of consensual sex or intimacy among adults, and it should extend to encompass all behaviors and to include children. Similarly, the term *bodily autonomy* tends to be more widely recognized as part of a specific topic: reproductive justice advocacy—more specifically, the pro-choice abortion rights movement. To extend these important concepts beyond the scope of sex and reproduction, let's look how parents' mistakes around bodily autonomy can contradict the practice of consent culture among children. When children don't feel sure about inappropriate touch, we must look at the narratives around body ownership and consent. This is why we have to look at confident bodily autonomy for all people, even before they become adults and outside of the context of sex.

Mistake no. 1: Teaching Children to Ignore Personal Boundaries

In the US, we have a subtle history of showing children that their bodies are owned by their parents. Forced physical contact with relatives reinforces the dangerously wrong message that relatives can't be abusers. "Grandpa just wants to hug you. Don't back away" and other similar verbal prompts tell children to ignore their feelings about a person (whether based on intuition or past experience) and listen to what an adult says instead.

As well-meaning observers, we adults often infringe on personal boundaries within children's interactions. Coercing a reserved child to hold hands and dance around with an outgoing child may feel like we're helping that child develop good social skills, but what we may actually be doing is teaching them that it's okay for other people to force them to do what makes those people (or other people) comfortable.

In later years, that can cause some children to feel that they need to be forced to do things, or that their natural tendency is somehow not okay. This can also have long-term negative effects on their social skills, because self-esteem and authentic friendships are difficult to form and maintain when a person isn't okay with who and how they innately are.

Also, many children who endure sexual abuse in particular don't tell, because they're afraid of being blamed for being complicit in the abuse. This tells us that children don't understand abuse. That's in part because we, the adults, don't give them the language to name these experiences and to feel safe coming to us about them.

Difficult aspects of personal boundary violation, particularly peer-to-peer abuse, make it extra complicated for adults to feel clear on how to broach the topic with children. But children need to know that other children can be abusers, and that they can abuse another child by touching them without permission, even if that child told them *yes* in the past.

Whether subtle or overt, the effects of childhood body violations are that we don't feel that we own ourselves. I know this from personal experience. We feel uncomfortable, unsure, or even afraid about asserting dominion over our own bodies.

Again, it's important to realize that our bodies and our boundaries exist outside of sex, and consent is required for anything having to do with our bodies. A solution to the blurred lines of personal boundaries is to practice parenting without coercion.

Consent culture should start with children—and when children grow up believing that all people have the right to control and protect their own bodies, then they're likely to respect other people's boundaries and to speak up when boundaries—whether their own or those of others—are being violated.

Mistake no. 2: Reinforcing Shame or Silence Around Body-Related Feelings

Instead of starting positive, developmentally appropriate conversation about bodies, sex, and intimacy in general, many parents tend to omit those terms when conversing with their children. But getting comfortable with saying penis, vagina, anus, or even the more popular (and maybe less easy to hear from a child) slang terms like *butthole*, for example, can lessen the feeling of shame around talking about private body parts or body-related feelings.

These types of conversations can also help children feel equipped to communicate with someone they trust if they are being sexually violated, for example. This way, we're not just giving them language about what's happening with them, we're also helping them express what's happening *to* them.

If they're comfortable naming them, then they have language to utilize when those body parts are affected by anyone in any way.

Another word that often goes unspoken by parents to children in healthy ways is *masturbation*. It's normal for children's curiosity to include their own bodies, sometimes showing up as self-pleasuring. Labeling that form of self-exploration as bad or avoiding the topic with your child altogether can make it difficult for a child to feel comfortable with their own bodies and physical feelings. As caring adults, one way we can nurture safe space for children is to educate ourselves on taboo topics like masturbation and children, particularly prepubescent children.

Some of us may have incorrect ideas about masturbation based on our parents' perspectives or other aspects of our own introduction to sexuality. But our children are not us, and though they are our responsibility, their bodies and experiences are their own. In support of that, we can read, discuss, and watch our way toward a sex-positive approach to parenting, so that our children feel safe asking questions and knowing (from experience) that they can discuss any aspect of their bodies with us, including sensations and thoughts that they may find pleasurable. Personally, I address masturbation with my daughters in part because I don't ever want to set the precedent that anyone (not even their mother) needs to validate how they explore aspects of their sexuality.

My intention is to avoid making masturbation an issue of morality or appropriateness, and instead to focus on what is socially safe and personally hygienic. In other words, as Lea Grover so perfectly stated, "We don't play with our vulvas at the table."

Mistake no. 3: Neglecting to Teach Your Child the Importance of Their Intuition

Intuition is not exclusive to adulthood, and it can play a very important role in helping a child develop a healthy sense of bodily autonomy. At any age, we have feelings in our bellies or chests, for example, that are directly triggered a sense of safety or lack thereof. Help children to name and acknowledge those feelings— and to trust them.

One way I practice nurturing intuition is to help children understand what intuition does. For my girls, I like the simple definition of intuition as a kind of internal safety alarm. I give them specific examples of times that I listened to my intuition and kept myself safe and times that I ignored my intuition and wasn't sure how to protect myself when I faced danger.

I'm not always sure if this is effective, but it helps me be sure that I'm practicing what I believe will work and what has worked with them in prior instances.

Asking them how intuition feels for them is good too. That way, they've verbalized the feelings and can more easily recognize and even share them when they show up.

Some parents tend to direct their child on how they should interact with a new adult, instead of watching and seeing how their child responds to that adult and going from there. That's an example of intuitive interference. For a child to develop a sense of trust in their own intuition, we as parents have to respect their choices and decide on a safe place and time to discuss the inter-action and see if our child has questions. This is where we parents can be advocates and allies of our children.

For example, if I meet up with a friend who has an outgoing child, and I have my bona fide introvert in tow, I let that parent know that my daughter may or may not play with their child, and that she may not hug them or participate in any well-meaning small talk.

I often bring books, games, and even art supplies along so that my daughter can feel comfortable when she accompanies me somewhere, without feeling pushed to engage with anyone, child or adult, unless she chooses to do so.

You can also tell them about your own experiences with intui-tion and encourage them to talk, write about, or act out moments when they recognized intuitive feelings. When we parent without addressing intuitive feelings and how to express them, we can miss opportunities to convey the importance of words like "no" and "stop" or phrases like "I don't want to" or "I don't like that."

If a child is playing with someone whose body language or verbal cues make that child feel uncomfortable, we can tell them that an uneasy feeling in their belly or chest is enough to warrant them saying "no," "stop," or "I don't like that," because their bodies are their own, and they get to choose what is done to it.

And more than that, they get to express their choice through consent or refusal.

Also tell them that it's important they stop whatever they're doing to someone else's body when that person uses those key terms. This way, we help children to start exploring the reality that they may not agree with or understand why someone is saying "no" to them, but the person does not need to explain why they're declining whatever they're declining.

Saying "no" is enough.

There are examples in all parts of the world of lack of consent where children are concerned. Certainly, this includes sexual abuse, which is the normal focus around consent culture, but it also it includes more than that. It also includes non-sexual activities and daily occurrences that offer opportunity to practice consent culture in all aspects of living. The point here is to become much more proactive about preventing sexual and other forms of physical abuse of children by adults, and among children as well. We may not be able to prevent all instances, but if we raise young people who are clear about personal boundaries and armed with the language and clarity about their feelings and bodily rights, then we can minimize these instances, as well as the harm done by them. And we can stop the cycle of children who become adults wrestling with unresolved pain and trauma because their bodies were not treated as their own property.

CHAPTER FIVE

Birth of a Postcolonial Perspective on Parenting

I sat there, legs crossed, palms sweaty, smile fake as ever, mind trying to look engaged in the combination of small talk and directives the producers and show host were giving us. The sleeves on the green dress the wardrobe dude and I had finally agreed on was sticking to my underarms and threatening to out my nervousness on national television. I was among nine people on that stage, four of us on each of the two panels and our moderator, the host of the show Mr. Steve Harvey. His humor and warmth put me somewhat at ease, but that didn't last long, because a few minutes into our talk, I saw that the setup was an Us versus Them scenario. And the Us—me and three other parents who identified as unschoolers—were viewed as the fools whose children would never amount to anything, mine most of all, because they were Black children, and, in America, Black adults, let alone their children, were not at liberty to be all free-spirited and natural learning–minded; it just wasn't feasible in the context of the systemic racism that historically stifled, targeted, and violated Black families, and still does today.

A friend who is a former journalist referred me to the producers of a daytime television show about unconventional parenting. That's how, in March 2016, I ended up on NBC's *The Steve Harvey Show*, and that's how I met Toya Graham. Toya is the woman who was widely known across America for knocking her teenage son Michael Singleton upside the head and berating him for being present at the Baltimore uprising following the death of twenty-five-year-old Baltimore resident Freddie Gray, who died after sustaining injuries during an arrest and transfer to jail by Baltimore police. Toya was on the "Them" side of the panel, and though she and I had extremely different views on parenting, I saw myself in Toya. More specifically, I saw that Toya and I had the same fears about our Black children not being educated on the realities of being Black in America—a responsibility that I, as their mother, clearly had on my shoulders. And having spoken with Kris about this, I knew he shared my fears.

Through her brash comments and adamant stance, Toya Graham helped me see that my fears could never guarantee my daughters' safety. And more than that, acting on those fears through the use of physical violence would stand to separate my children from me in ways that would only lessen their safety. I had already watched the video of Toya and her son, and, later, as I sat on that panel with Toya mere feet away from me explaining her rationale for repeatedly slapping and pushing her son, even as he tried to walk away, I recognized her choice as one that could no longer work for me. I have the luxury of not having had Toya's specific experience, but hearing her in person allowed me to truly see a mother beat on a child out of what she called love and realize that I had hit my daughters out of that same love in the past. And I had been wrong. If Marley and Sage could not trust me to move past fear and treat them like people not property, then they would have every right to lie to me about where they were, what they were doing, and why they were doing it.

I left NBC's Chicago studios feeling really clear on the ways that fear and learned behaviors were causing me to operate outside my beliefs in equity for all people, especially children. And when Kris and I sat down to reevaluate our stance on hitting our daughters, we both got clear that hitting them was no longer an option.

If our fears for our children's safety caused us to treat them in the very same ways we hope they will not be treated by others, what was the point? How were they safe, then? And how were we justified in using tools of oppression, violence in particular, in our efforts to raise our children as liberated, confident people?

We weren't justified. We were mimicking the ways that we were raised, and we hadn't questioned or examined the why behind both of our upbringings and whether or not we wanted to carry those fears into our own approach to parenting. We spoke to Marley and Sage about our decision to never hit them again. We explained ourselves in detail, and we apologized for the choices we made and asked them to trust us to start making better choices around discipline. We held to that decision and are still examining how our past as part of a people who had been colonized is affecting our present.

Since that realization, I've also come to see that much of my anxiety around Marley and Sage's behaviors wasn't even about how I felt about their actions; it was about how other people might view me as a result of the girls' behaviors—that same performance work I called the adult gaze earlier. Indeed, since so much of adulthood is weighed by how in control of the children entrusted to us we seem be, Marley and Sage endured the pressure of perception right alongside the standard judgment and fear-based view of children by their parents. Recognizing is the easy part; replacing those old habits with new norms is the work.

That wasn't the first time a conversation led me to wrestle with the connection between my personal approach to parenting and society's influence over my relationship with my children. The first time was a few months before Sage was born, when my then supervisor (let's call her Lisa), a brilliant chemist who was also mothering a Black girl, said something that rooted itself in my very soul. Lisa's father was Black and her mother Japanese. She and I talked about womanhood, mothering, cultural differences, and wrestling with ideas of the American Dream, and sometimes we talked about discipline. Lisa was the first person I'd heard connect hitting a child to what she called *slave master behavior*. I don't remember her exact words, but I will never forget how they made me feel. What I took from her words was that as Black people, we hit our children because we were hit as children, and that our great-grandparents were hit by owners of enslaved people, and that it was not our norm to hit our children before that. It was a mechanism for dealing with the warped reality that someone owned your child, and that you had to thwart any behavior that resembled (a false sense of) freedom from your child or otherwise put them at risk of being hurt, sold, or killed. Shittery, shit, shit, shittt.

I nearly fell out of my chair as Lisa's words made their way through my mind. I never researched this to see if there was written evidence or whatever—didn't need to. Her message was for me either way, and it nestled itself in my psyche, demanding that I begin to seriously question my violence toward my children. I had already had Marley, was pregnant with Sage, and though I heard and felt Lisa's words, I still thought it was probably a bad idea to not give a child the "reality of the consequences of their actions." Her words gave me pause, and I did begin to question my norm, but my old habits of control and power were easier to listen to back then. I didn't write it out, like I usually need to do when I'm truly processing something. At that point, I just questioned a few things in my mind and mostly made excuses for why I chose what I chose. Lisa was talking about violent beatings; I was just talking about slaps and other hits that came with explanations, which in my mind, made it better, more humane somehow. Thankfully, as my relationships with my daughters emerged, I began seeing them as people not property, people who I could consider being mine but also owning themselves, I learned to pivot toward healthy dynamics and away from control-driven ones. Still, it took more than a decade, until I met Toya Graham in 2016, for it to connect with me enough to change my behavior, not just my thoughts but my actions.

When Toya attacked her son, she was giving him a version of something he would survive, whereas the police would give him something final. It was her job to put that fear in her boy, because we know, historically, that the white people in charge of everyone's supposed safety had their own ways of putting fear into Black bodies, be they boys, girls, non-binary, grown, young, or elder. I saw a connection between my old supervisor's words and Toya's actions. For many Black people, keeping our children and our neighbors' children in line and out of the way of the powers that be is how we helped each other survive. And, later, our education, particularly since the world of academia was fully vetted in its whiteness, was how we dared to go even beyond survival. Just as children are groomed to show up, both at home and in public, in ways that make adults comfortable, Black folks in the countries I grew up in, Jamaica and America, have also been groomed to show up in ways that make the people who are in positions of greater power than us . . . comfortable—socially this means White people. That performance for the comfort of and in response to the perceived threats by the powers that be is a major reason that my mother, for example, would glare at my brother and me if we so much as spoke in an octave above a whisper inside our local bank. As Black children, we needed to show good White folks that we could behave, and that we could keep our Blackness to ourselves, where it belonged.

School is perceived to be the space where Black children, non-Black Indigenous children, and the children of People of Color (collectively, BIPOC children) could use those performance techniques to get on a so-called level playing field with White people. This is why for many families of color, the term unschooling is unsettling and even offensive, because education is, after all, linked to liberation. And though this is (in some cases) true, it cannot be viewed as a sweeping truth, because the realities of what many BIPOC children endure at the hands of schooling ain't got nothin' to do with liberation and everything to do with the evolution of colonization and, in the case of the school-to-prison pipeline, is a thoroughly effective feeder into modern-day slavery. Turns out that BIPOC children don't even have to be in school to be attacked by police; I know firsthand from my teenage years growing up in South Florida that my body, my presence, was viewed as a threat, and the expectation was for me to perform a type of subservience and fear-based communication to appear less threatening to White people, in this case, a policeman.

Four friends and I were walking home from our middle school dance; I was fourteen years old. It was around 9:00 p.m. We were in our own neighborhood, and all of us, except for my friend's big brother (our designated walk-home-chaperone), were middle school students. A few minutes into our walk, a police car drove up, and the officer behind the wheel asked us where we were going. We said "home" in unison and sped up our pace, as we were accustomed to doing when we saw the notoriously racist White police in our predominantly Black, South Florida city. He drove alongside us and asked us more questions. We stopped answering because we knew better than to talk to the police. In response, he hastily parked his vehicle in our walking path and spilled out of his car, his eyes narrow and his chest high. His questions continued, and I asked him why he had driven his car onto the sidewalk, why he had pulled out his flashlight and shine it in our faces on the well-lit street. The next thing I knew, all 105 pounds of my body was hurled against the hood of his car. That officer did not see a student or a little girl, he saw a Black person and handled me accordingly. My right arm was twisted behind my back, and his left hand, in which he also held a flashlight, was against the back of my head so that my face would stay pressed against the car's hot hood. My friend's big brother pled with the officer to let me get up from the front of the car. I yelled that the heat from the hood was burning my face, and that he was going to break my arm. He tightened his grip, yelled at our chaperone in between hurling words at the rest of us Eventually, begrudgingly, he let me up. We all ran in silence, each dispersing in the direction of our house. I don't even know how I got home, because I was so frightened and out of sorts that I was not even sure I was running in the right direction. My ears were ringing, I'm pretty sure that I had urinated on myself, and I wasn't sure how my mother would react to what had happened.

When I got home and told my mother what happened, she was so angry and adamant that she even seemed angry with me! She was angry that her daughter had been violated. She was angry that I didn't get the officer's badge number. And she was angry that she could not stop it from probably happening again—not to her daughter, not to one of her sons, and not to any other Black person daring to be happy and human while living in America. Violence against Black bodies, and against all non-White-presenting bodies, is so normal in Western society that some Black people, myself included, internalized that shit, adopted it, and used it, along with school, as means through which we hoped to groom and educate our way out from under the tyranny of systemic, sordid white supremacy. I know firsthand that this "because if I don't they will," fear-based punishment will not protect my children from those set on doing them harm. I know from later conversations with my children how I compromised trust and respect in our relationship by being violent to them. Those conversations, coupled with those memories, along with the dots Kris and I connected through my assessment of Toya's experience, cemented the new normal; we were never going to hit our children again.

We were never going to hit our children again. I had reframed what it meant to explore discipline with my children, which rooted our respect-based parenting practice even more, this time addressing issues of bodily autonomy that went way beyond whether or not our girls had to wear bras. I began addressing my own recollection of times when my young-girl body didn't feel safe, like the incident with that South Florida policeman. Surely, what Kris and I were doing at home wasn't the same thing, but it certainly sat inside the same beliefs. I saw that unschooling wasn't just about my daughters but was also about my participation in a way of being in the world and about being honest that I, just like that Broward County cop, was using my position of legal and physical power over a person to frighten them into doing what made me comfortable. As their parent, I was acclimating my daughters to violence from a loved one, which meant they could reasonably expect other people who loved them to be physically violent with them. At that point, Kris and I questioned our options for responding to the moments when we felt our daughters were out of line: Didn't children who weren't afraid of their parents end up as entitled, spoiled, ill-adjusted adults? What was the respect-based way to deal with our daughters' instances of resistance?

These particular questions led me to look at the history of the ways certain groups of people's bodies had been colonized. The ways that my own people's bodies were perceived as land that was to be groomed and used for the benefit of the people in power and not regarded as worthy of respect simply because they were the bodies of human beings. Instead, in practice, those human bodies were viewed as and reduced to bodies that worked as those in power saw fit. Now, the questions I thought and wrote about looked more like this: What were Kris and I forcing our daughters to do for us to be comfortable and them to be impressive?

I began to reframe parenting, and this is when I began seeing and proclaiming my parenting as part of my intersectional feminist practices. In June 2016, I wrote a piece about intersectional feminist parenting (it was published on Ravishly.com). Here's an excerpt:

> My beliefs about people's rights, including my own, are a significant factor in how I define myself, how I

identify, and how I treat other people. And since I am, in fact, raising people, my approach to parenting must reflect those beliefs too. Otherwise, I risk robbing my daughters of the same sense of personal agency and social responsibility that I believe promotes more confidence and compassion among people in the world. Our society treats children as a group that cannot be trusted and that needs to be guided, usually through punishment, physical violence, forced education, and little to no input into how they spend the majority of their time. I disagree wholeheartedly, and I don't want to perpetuate that narrative. Essentially, I see intersectional feminist parenting as a solution to the lack of spaces where young people can build confident autonomy in all aspects of their lives—even when their choices and lifestyle go against the beliefs, power, and inherent privilege of the adults in their lives. I'm talking about resisting the power and privileging of adulthood over youth (which some people call "adultism"). Parents who identify as feminist or as supporters of feminist parenting have different means of applying this idea to their everyday choices. The life topics are pretty similar, though—body positivity and autonomy, open communication, embracing diversity, practicing compassion and respect for oneself and others, doing away with gender-based roles, and embodying confident self-expression.

One month after I published that piece, undue police violence against Black people would affect my life yet again. This time, it wasn't my physical body that was attacked, it was the bodies of two other innocent people, men who were partners, fathers, and loved/loving members of their community. Their deaths were widely publicized, and the message behind their deaths further internalized by many of us: we are not safe, our children are not safe, there is no safe space, and, therefore, no real freedom, if you are Black in America. Because my body is not behind bars or contracted to a place that drains my mental energy all day, I don't experience myself as enslaved. I am definitely dependent on modern conveniences and am not living off grid growing my own food, but I am free. I *am* free, and I also know freedom always costs something. In a legal system molded at the hands of forefathers who did not see non-White people as human, as trustworthy, as having a right to life, liberty, and all that, I have to deliberately carve out my postcolonial life. Reason being, everything ain't post-colonial! Legal processes, academic structures, the medical industry, all examples of far-reaching industries still rooted in and governed by written word and expressed sentiments mirror those of the most effective of colonizing nations.

Seen through the conventional parenting lens, the one most of us raised in Western culture think about when we think of parents, children don't just become adults, they get molded into adulthood—responsible adulthood if the adults that own them do right by them. Seen through the adult-centric lens, children are widely viewed as beautiful but soft clay to be molded into a responsible adult status. To *not* mold a child is to neglect them, to shirk one's responsibility. Our children are ours, legally and morally; we are in charge of them. As such, we're responsible for giving them the best step-up into adulthood that we can manage to eke out. Looking through that lens, one could summarize that we own children, and we owe them. What we mainly owe them is a good education. And, somehow, that does not require their approval or input, because our adulthood qualifies us to decide on their behalf until they reach age eighteen.

Postcolonial parenting showed up for me as part of my deschooling journey. It speaks to my need to examine, question, and confront what I've accepted as normal parenting practices, so that I can see the ways some of them are reactions to being part of a group of people who were colonized and whose identities and beliefs were and are shaped by white supremacy, and who are, therefore, emotionally, spiritually, and physically harmful. The term made and makes sense to me, because it says, simply, how I parent is heavily informed by my decolonization work. To raise my children as free people, I need to be versed in freedom. I need to recognize it, know when it is threatened, and trust myself to act on what I know. If I viewed my children as fertile land to shape and design without the partnership of their own choices and curiosities, then I would be colonizing that land, those children. I would be the oppressor in this instance, just as I was when Kris and I stood by the school system instead of Marley and Sage. Postcolonial parenting is my assembling of the scaffolding I will continue to need as I learn more about the ways colonization has affected me personally, as well as the ways I affect the people and environments around me. If I am ignorant to the harm I'm causing, then I will keep causing it. Just like I kept hitting my children until meeting Toya Graham helped me consider if and how my parenting was being informed by some shit I didn't even believe—that hitting children does more good than harm. I went back to that slave master behavior theory Lisa had shared with me back when I was pregnant with Sage. The imprint of the level of fear instilled in my great-great-grand whoever influenced subsequent generations so deeply that I was holding those same fears and resulting actions, without questioning them. I was now responsible for decolonizing my relationships, starting with myself and my children.

Viewing my relationships with Marley and with Sage as postcolonial allows me to go beyond adult-centric ideas of what it means to mother or to parent. It reminds me of the need to consider Marley and Sage as their own sovereign land, still needing Kris and me for some things but never needing to be controlled. Sometimes needing to be guided, dissuaded, hugged, reminded, forgiven, seen, heard but never needing to be controlled. It was not my intention to acclimate two more women on this planet to oppression—not two Black women, at that! Postcolonialism as a lens, a reference point, is, at this stage in my deschooling, incredibly helpful.

Today, I realize that the effects of Philando's and Alton's murders—the impact of the losses of those two men in their families and communities—catalyzed a level of activism in my life by way of messages from Black families all across America about whether or not we and our children could ever be free and what it might cost us to get there. I'm not saying these discussions are new, I am saying they were new for *me*, especially because more people seemed willing to talk about this out loud, repeatedly, and with solutions, not only venting, but as part of shaping the intended outcomes. Now, more people were adamant that they couldn't surrender their children to toxic schools, for reasons that included but went beyond Whitewashed curricula and over into the ways their children were being forced to internalize their own degradation. People, not just parents, were afraid and angry, and people were also ready to do more than acknowledge the ongoing influence of colonization. They—we—were willing to do, and in some cities, were already doing, something toward that freedom. And what we were doing was deepening our decolonization work by examining and working through the ways that colonization was still informing the people who helped raise us, as well as our own actions and fears. Change was not only due, it was being called in, drummed in, loud and insistent, and I gathered myself and my resources to set out to amplify these voices of change and remind more people that we could figure out how to get free, if we first stopped tapping into the tools of oppression that had been forced into the hands of people before us and would be forced into ours, unless we intentionally let them go.

CHAPTER SIX

Recognizing Unschooling as a Communal Model for Collective, Long-Term Liberation

Their text messages read like they were written with urgency. Papas, mamas, and aunties messaged me with their wonderings about whether tucking their children inside classrooms would make them less threatened by those who targeted them. Single mothers typed with fury about being part of good, strong homeschooling co-ops but wondering if they should put their children in schools, because these homeschooling field trips, for example, might make their children easier targets. I heard from somebody's daddy who feared that his daughter might feel *too free* and would, therefore, be ill-equipped to perform in the ways America preferred—providing a space of reverence and gratitude that made White people more comfortable around us. During that tragic summer of 2016 for Alton and Philando, many of us raged inside and among ourselves. Of course and unfortunately, the circumstances under which these Black men were killed were not abnormal in America. Our family had had several conversations about the reality of modern-day lynchings and how that affected the way we moved around in public, feeling a realistic and justified fear of authorities but also determined to own ourselves and embrace our right to be visible, to find joy, and to feel free. Philando and Alton weren't killed because of school; they were killed because of anti-Black beliefs and actions. Here are some questions that came up for me:

- Since, historically, Black people were not free to move about America without risking being killed and still aren't today, how in the world could anyone raising a Black child see their child as free, let alone free to follow their own educational paths like Kris and I were claiming to do?
- What would happen when they were walking around in neighborhoods engaging in life learning? Who would keep them safe?
- What were the fears and the costs of raising a liberated Black person?
- What about White people raising Black children? Would they be able to recognize and address the ways people of color must navigate whiteness?
- Was unschooling a "White thing" that only White people could do, the same way Black awareness in Jamaica was often viewed as something only counterculture movements or well-off families could speak on and live out?
- How could I be calling for liberation to extend to children in the form of unschooling when, clearly, we were not free?

When our daughters were twelve and ten, and I remember talking with Kris about how Marley was the same age as Tamir Rice when he was gunned down in Ohio by local police. We weren't the only parents having these realizations. After Alton and Philando were murdered, parents of children of varying ages messaged me about their own internal realizations and resulting conflicts. They, like Kris and me sometimes, wondered how we could endeavor to raise our children as free people who felt comfortable expressing themselves in the world when there were White people who targeted people like our children—and us—for no other reason than the fact that we were Black and outside. Aiyana Stanley-Jones wasn't even outside her home when, in 2010, her little body was invaded by bullets from police officer's guns. We could list name after name, mourn body after Black body, and all that naming and mourning made us feel less and less safe with ideas like unschooling, for fear that they may be too lofty a vision for us to sustain inside the harsh, pervasive reality of white supremacy and its inherent violence. I responded to folks as quickly as I could, but the emails and direct messages kept coming. I felt like I needed to respond in a way that would serve more of us and that would serve us consistently, not just in a moment of fear. I recognized that Black and Brown folks needed to remember why our children deserve to live as people, not just people performing studenthood. I decided to speak out loud about our collective right to freedom and, more so, to make space for more families of color to speak out loud about the ways they were claiming their freedom through unschooling. It was clear that this means of shifting from oppression to empowerment with our daughters was not something we were doing alone. Many other families were doing this; communities all over America were invested in this, and we needed to know about each other, to hear from each other, to face our fears and nurture our healing together.

That summer, from a sense of urgency, anger, and intention to push past some serious liberation hurdles, I started recording and publishing conversations with other unschoolers. I started *Fare of the Free Child* podcast to help amplify the underrepresented voices and unique concerns of Black people, non-Black Indigenous people, and People of Color (BIPOC) families seeking real, viable options to the oppressive systems within which our children were expected to live and to learn. The space was meant to explore and celebrate BIPOC life that was neither centered on the White gaze nor the performance of our children within dominant White culture. We needed to see that choosing an option like unschooling was not something each of us was doing alone. We needed to hear about the ways that communities were formed and strengthened through families' efforts to raise free people and to free themselves from ideas steeped in white supremacy,

ideas about schooling and capitalism. What I had seen as my
personal work, first for my daughters, and then for myself,
was public now. It was political. It was communal. It was a
matter of honoring the people who came before me, and who
lived and died so that I could actually be free. It turns out that
so many people were feeling these feelings, and this chapter
will talk about the responses to the podcast and the resulting
communities that formed or expanded when folks found out
about each other through the podcast.

I knew from experience, that some people would hear
my podcast and its focus on BIPOC families and take issue
with that. That didn't matter to me. It was Black bodies on
those streets, it was Black children in those caskets, and it
has been Black and Brown people of all ages, backgrounds,
and socioeconomic classes whose children were seen as haz-
ardous and less than human; we needed to speak about it
among ourselves, as ourselves, and that's what I set out to
do and have been doing in collaboration with thousands of
listeners since then.

I started *Fare of the Free Child* for all of us—for BIPOC
families reeling from fear and fury and love. I started it for
BIPOC children determined to get their parents' attention
and talk about their options, the way my daughters had to
do with Kris and me. I started it with the expectation of conversation and change, but what I didn't know is that my little
podcast would also create community. The conversations
were so good and so thorough, and we were hungry for them.
I was never lacking for guests, topics, or listeners. I could feel
the connection as folks tuned in, first every other week, and
then (because there was so much to cover) weekly. In those
first two seasons, we talked about the basics of unschooling
with parents whose children had never been in school and,
of course, taught themselves all kinds of things that most of
us, myself included, had thought could only happen by direct
instruction that was probably involuntary on the child's part.
We had on a busy, full-time, nine to five–plus environmental

volunteer of a mama who was struggling to find community even with a Self-Directed Education (SDE) center in her city. One of the main barriers for her family was that variations in cultural needs did not go away just because there were similarities in the parents' ideas that children should be free to learn, and, like many other non-White families, the implicit bias factor affected her children in ways that it did not affect White children, because systemic and structural racism are part of the childcare world too. We talked about that on several episodes. We (because FOFC listeners are so present for me that it feels like we, not I, talk with each guest) talked to entrepreneurs who incorporated unschooling and deschooling methods into the way the they lived, and, as a result, grew their businesses and brought their families closer together when they released the reins on their children's educational paths and freed them from school and from school at home. We talked about the unschooling movement in South Africa and how it was directly influenced by deliberate decolonization efforts among families and larger communities, how they were reimagining learning through a postcolonial lens. No doubt, that influenced my lens. We talked about self-love and making sacred space to deal with the inner work and triggers that stomp through all the spaces when we commit to raising free people. We unpacked legal systems and single motherhood. We talked about present Black fathers and Latinx cultural values that align with deschooling. We talked to parents who started and grew learning centers in their own communities, some called Sudbury schools or Democratic schools, others Agile Learning Centers (ALC), a network of Self-Directed Education spaces that use variations of a model I appreciate and will talk more about shortly. We talked about the relationship drama and the healing that comes with deciding not to perform conventional parent-child dynamics but, instead, to learn to be your authentic selves together. So many details that went beyond the question of what type of school or not-school a child should attend or whether they were falling behind someone or something. We talked about the real deal with college, why it is not the best option for every young person, and what they might do with self-direction in mind instead of the unexamined grade school to college path.

Fare of the Free Child podcast started out as a thing I'd do on the side. A couple times a month, I'd blast out a message from a person who had already starting shifting to more partner-centered relationships with their children and felt good about how things were progressing. I'd also speak directly to the fears folks expressed in those emails when I didn't have a guest. What I didn't count on was the podcast becoming central in my life. All my writing was about the same conversations I was having with folks on the podcast or because of the podcast. People were saying I was giving language to what they'd been feeling but had not been able to put to words. My writing pitches started getting accepted more often, because I was talking about unschooling and raising free people with a focus that intersects with other aspects of civil rights and social justice work. I stopped making time for pitching, because I needed to just write and speak and interview and study and do my work in my own house and in my own spirit. I stopped pitching essays and just focused on supporting the people reaching out through the podcast—and on letting all this work *work* me. I was walking my talk with my daughters and my choices, and maybe this ain't nothing new to you, but, for me, this is the type of work that undoes and rebuilds your life, because it is messy, vital life design work.

As I lived my truth out loud and studied it out loud and in community with other parents and longtime, self-described "recovering educators," I started to feel the sense of community that was forming and see the network of people raising free people. It also nurtured (and still nurtures) Kris's and my relationships with Marley and Sage. The podcast became an important relationship in my life, and I let it arrange me and my life. I listened and read responses from people who said a guest on the podcast changed their whole life, and that they needed to hear *me* say the things I said, just the way I said them, because hearing those things episode after episode got them to the mindset of finally trusting themselves or their child, which meant making some major life shifts. I could not stop. I began to feel more connected to my ancestors and often imagined (and still imagine) sitting in counsel with them, being entrusted as one of the voice workers who knew to speak far and wide about repairing the intergenerational fissures that came with our colonization. I really could not stop. There were too many questions that we ask out loud that needed to be answered. Twice a month became three times a month. Then weekly, sometimes more. It was pouring out from cities all over the US. I started expanding my understanding of the obstacles to liberation that went beyond education.

Perhaps, most surprisingly, plenty of White people kept emailing me saying, "Thank you for speaking honestly. I can see that there are, in fact, things I can do to support BIPOC around me," and that a lot of what they heard through the podcast conversations applied to them too. We were learning together; I felt like I built an amplifier for what many of us needed and were, in many cases, doing and could now feel a real sense of community around. I remember one particular mama had me in tears when she left me a heartfelt message about how she found out about homeschooling co-ops through the podcast, and that turned into the community they needed to finally rescue their children from all that was happening to them in schools. Steadily, an outpouring of responses came through from listeners of all races and nationalities. People told me how they had been fighting through those same questions and feelings. They poured out their hearts about being ostracized by family members for choosing to live without a focus on school. Others still had children in school and were feverishly working to find solutions to the coercive nature of schooling and the social issues it magnified, preserved, and perpetuated. Others had already started to solve their school wound woes with by forming SDE cooperatives, informal groups, intentional learning communities, and liberatory in-home family practices. I was surprised, because, like many of the people who found my podcast, I had felt like my family was the only one in our newly designed world; I am so glad I was wrong! Families all over the world, including Jamaica, Japan, South Africa, Nigeria, Kenya, Sweden, Croatia, Australia, Colombia, among others, had families and extended communities that had already opted out of problematic schooling and were spending their days together, children and adults, inside and outside their homes, recognizing and supporting natural learning. Much of what I was learning about how these collectives formed had to do with unmet cultural needs. Indigenous families in Tucson, Arizona, helped to create SDE spaces that valued the intersection of race, identity, and culture. Unschoolers showed up in their identities: Black people, Latinx people, White people, and folks from all nationalities and religious beliefs left me direct messages and detailed voice messages about their parenting-related liberation efforts.

Shortly after the launching of *Fare of the Free Child*, Donald Trump became America's president and, once again, I experienced a significant increase in the outpouring of people reaching out to me about a specific event in our shared recent history. This time, it was an ever-growing population of White parents talking about their fears; they didn't want to raise another racist White person like the one who was now at America's helm, and they didn't know how to proceed. All of us were clear about wanting to raise children differently than in the ways that were promoted by conventional education, society, and parenting practices. We all wanted and were actively seeking out spaces to create language and practices needed to develop the tools of liberation—social justice, mindful relationships, and collaborative, intentional, self-directed, self-organizing practices that can be applied at home and in group/community settings. As caregivers, we all wanted our children to make decisions that didn't get in the way of other people's right to be free, safe, and happy. We shared an intention to take responsibility for our roles in helping to raise children who were not blind to injustice, bias, or systemic issues, and who were confident in their efforts to help shift the world away from the oppressive one they inherited from us. Those shared intentions and desires create the conditions for the essentials of unschooling to emerge. Those essentials, that structure, can look like being at home together, or it can look like young people being dropped off and picked up from an all-day, self-directed group thing, facilitated by adults who believe in and commit to practicing unschooling and deschooling methods as part of how they work and play with young learners. Whether at home or in a larger SDE group space, the adult's role is to clear the way for each child's natural learning path to emerge and take a shape that we are equipped to recognize.

Adults must also be trustworthy, so that children know they can invite support and guidance and still be seen and treated like the driver not the passenger on their learning journey. Our job is not to put things in children's environments "so they can learn" but to establish clear conditions for observing and subsequently supporting each child's emergent learning structure. And as we allow for the broadening of unschooling beyond education to the details of everyday living together, we begin to deschool—to shed the programming and habits that grew out of other people having agency (control) over our time, body, thoughts, or actions. This is where we start to get in a rhythm; this is when, and perhaps *how*, healing begins to happen and becomes inextricably linked to deschooling.

Fare of the Free Child, Episode 0

All children deserve to be free, and certainly there are parents of all races and backgrounds who are already doing radical and necessary work to promote and protect the rights of children through the Self-Directed Education movement. I'm here for all of that, and I've benefited from much of what they have done and are doing— Carol Black, Peter Gray, John Holt, Charles Eisenstein, Pat Farenga, and, more recently, Anna Brix Thomsen and those amazing folks.

This podcast, though, will center Black and Brown voices, because, in this Self-Directed Education movement, when you search it online or see it in media or go to an event, there is a blatant absence of diversity, of Black and Brown faces and voices and concerns. Because our ability to take our children out of school or keep them out of school has other factors to it than just willingness and money.

As a member of the Black diaspora, I see and know the reality that people who look like me are being dehumanized, oppressed, silenced, and overtly exploited by white supremacy, by capitalism, by the effects of colonialism, on a global and consistent scale. While White parents are focused on the rights their children should have, Black and Brown people are worried about the safety of our children.

It is those voices, the ones who are both afraid and brave, and the ones who have ideas on how to live and thrive despite these legitimate fears, that *Fare of the Free Child* aims to amplify. Because, as writer and organizer Malkia Cyril so beautifully put it, "There are no voiceless people, only those that haven't yet been heard."

I want to use this space to create community for adults engaged in unconventional Black and Brown parenting and caregiving to be heard and to find and support each other. And since I'm an unschooling, location independent, non-Christian, Caribbean, intersectional feminist, mermaid identifying, radical self-expression practicing, Blackity-Black woman and mother, raising two super-dope Black girls with my man, I am just the one to invite you into this conversation.

I also want to address the myth that if we give our children freedom, they're gonna lose their minds and slap us in the face like that kid on Dr. Phil or call us bitches in the supermarket when we don't buy them the cereal they want. A lot of us really see it that way, so we hold on to old thinking, out of reverence for our culture, to the detriment of our children. And then there are some of us who have figured out what to leave behind and what to build upon, but we struggle with the effects of the limited understanding of family members and friends in our communities who see our unconventional parenting style as a threat to our children or to our culture.

The reality is that treating children with more dignity and making more space for them to learn how to lead themselves and make real decisions about their own lives in childhood does not automatically increase your chances of having a child who is gonna disrespect you or themselves or see you as anything less than you are.

The reality is that each of us can decide exactly what we will hold on to in our culture and our history. And we can also decide that the parts of our tradition and our culture that do not resonate with who we are as individuals and how we want to connect as parents can be shed, without shame, and with support and understanding. This is a space for people of color to figure out how we and our children can live and thrive alongside a system that makes it clear that if you are not White, you are subject to terrorism at the hands of the same government to whom you pay taxes and to whom your children pledge their allegiance in their classrooms.

And, to be clear, I have an agenda. I want us to start treating our children with more dignity and giving them more autonomy over their own futures. And I want us to shift out of the thinking that this work of freeing children from oppressive structures is a White thing, as many Black folks keep telling me about unschooling in particular.

There's an entire spectrum in between free child and troubled child, so I know we see these kids on talk shows and in stores disrespecting their mamas and acting crazy and think, "Not my child." And I know we recognize that our children aren't privileged enough to act crazy in public and survive it. So we are fearful about our children's freedom, in large part because of the social, historical, and political contexts that show the lack of value on Black and Brown lives.

Still, we can't keep perpetuating this stifled, molded, narrow mindset when it comes to raising our children. They won't be prepared to own themselves and to thrive in a time where information is abundant and networking skills, language acquisition, and confident assertion will be critical to their survival. We have to figure this out together, without judging or bashing each other. So every other week we're gonna talk about all of that: the fears, the myths, the history, our history, the present, the future, and our communities. And we're talking about the things we can do, the action we can take, to start living in a more harmonious, more loving, more mindful, liberation-centered space with our young people today.

CHAPTER SEVEN

Leadership: The One-Word Bridge between Learning and Liberation

"Okay, so we go three blocks this way, make a right here, and then we can just follow the ocean along this path until we get to the restaurants on the left. Make that left and follow it for about five blocks, past the coconut water stand on the left, past the colorful hammock shop with all the seashells at the entrance, past the fish pedicure spa on the right, remember that place?"

"Yep," I responded. "What were those fish called? Gara something?" Sage was explaining to Kris and me what path she and Marley would walk if they had to go to the supermarket without us. One of the habits we developed over our years of travel was drawing maps. It started out as an assignment Kris would give the girls when we were in a new city, during our short homeschooling stint. We'd walk around our new complex and the neighborhood, and then we'd go back to our apartment or house, and Kris would ask the girls to map out a particular path, usually it was to the nearest food spot, be that a supermarket or a restaurant. It helped all of us feel safer, more knowledgeable about our new digs, and it felt schoolish, you know, *learn-y*, so we started doing it for those reasons at first, and then kept doing it, because it was fun and engaging, and, of course, useful in our getting to know wherever we were living.

"Yeah, so just go past the restaurant with the creepy giant lobster at the front," Marley picked up where Sage left off, "and past the other restaurant shaped like a tilted pirate ship; the supermarket will be on the right, across from that bike rental spot with the dude that looked just like Chevanni. Got it?"

"Nope." That was always my answer, because I usually just followed one of the girls or Kris until I got the lay of the land. I'm horrible with directions, and I admit that I rely on my family's appreciation for mapping things and knowing how to get to places, probably a lot more than I should. I've gotten a bit better, since being a digital nomad calls for all sorts of geography life lessons, but you'll never find me drawing maps for fun or sketching out pathways to grocery stores with a smile on my face. Thankfully, I neither have to like those things nor do them, because each of us is getting pretty good at staying in our lanes and trusting the resources around us and our own savvy to support us in getting what we needed in each city. Another deschooling mindset shift came in the form of my relationship to resources.

Before unschooling, I saw money as life's primary resource. Now, I see leadership as life's primary resource. When each of us, Kris, Sage, Marley, and I, are mindful about how we are leading ourselves and what we need to feel comfortable, collaboration based on each other's strengths and our collective trust of each other and ourselves is what renders all other resources usable or far less effective, be that money, time, access, or other people. Now, I see that people are resources, places are resources, conversations are resources, self-trust is a resource, and, yes, money is a resource, but not nearly as important as good personal leadership skills. Leadership, it turns out, is the piece I was working with but didn't really recognize the immense importance of, and this trip to the Pacific side of Costa Rica would hip Kris and me to the levels of personal leadership confidence that were developing in Marley and Sage.

Traveling wasn't a goal we had, it was a way of living within our means, because, for us, maintaining a home in the US was way more expensive, financially and emotionally, than short-term living in various cities across Jamaica and the US. Traveling was our way of exploring other parts of America and the world, so that the four of us could be more deliberate about where we wanted to live-live. When we first started, much like my schoolish mind wrestled with whether and how Marley and Sage could learn without school or textbooks, I also wondered when we could buy our next house and "get stable" again. Unlike my questions about learning, my questions around that were easily released, mainly because the more we traveled, the more I felt at home with myself. Deschooling shifted my mindset around being stable or settled to seeing *myself* not any physical place as home. Not even Jamaica was home in the same way for me anymore. I, as in my mind, soul, and physical body, am home. I. Am. Home. And I can live in many places, feel comfortable and safe and keep house in many places, as long as I am at home in myself, and my children and partner feel comfortable and safe where we lay our heads and make our meals. Traveling has brought us clarity about which cities and climates we enjoy most, and it has also helped us realize how few tangible things we need to feel at home—and, for me, how uncomfortable it was to be packed up with stuff that I didn't really need or use that often.

Minimalism—a lifestyle decision to live with fewer things and to only acquire or keep things that are deeply meaningful and useful in one's life—is another welcomed outcome from my deschooling journey. I went from stuffing extra pairs of shoes and pants into everyone else's luggage, to each of us traveling across continents for six months with no more than a carry-on bag and a personal item. Yes, I said six months. And yes, I said carry-on only. No checked bags, plenty of what we needed, and the freedom from excess shit that would literally and figuratively weigh us down. For me, minimalism is a meditation. It's mindfulness that calls me to it consistently, with just about every decision I make. I like having room in my backpack to find what I'm looking for when I stick my hand in there. I like having room in my carry-on to sort through all of it or to put extra bags of snacks in there, simply because I've got the space. But that six months with one bag experience was in 2018. Back in 2017, during our first trip to South Africa, we still each carried one personal item and a carry-on bag, but I was still part of the overstuffed luggage crew, sitting on my little red carry-on bag, trying to keep the zipper motivated to follow its tracks and keep it together, eyeing Kris's bag and feeling some kind of way that he wouldn't let me put just one more scarf in his empty-ass bag. Those are my travel gremlins talking; the parts of my mind that use snark and low-key saltiness to deal with the frustrating parts of airports, ticket agent apathy, definitive boarding times, and ever-reliable, always unnecessary, TSA sass (*Why you mad, bruh?*).

Traveling was also a way to give myself some distance between myself and all the people I loved who would directly, or indirectly, continually question my lifestyle choices and speak about their concerns about Marley's and Sage's whatever. I'm not a hold-my-tongue person, and I know how my responses can affect my children, not just me, and so the space to live and not navigate the feelings of explaining myself or not explaining myself was too much to add to the new stew. Africa, unlike overall travel, was a goal though, and Kris and I wanted to gift experience in Africa to Marley and Sage while they were young. We didn't want the whole continent to be some magical idea in their minds, like it was for us. We wanted them to know some of the countries, to hear some of the languages, to know firsthand that the perceptions of Africa as poor and backwards was fear-based, ignorant, biased bullshit. We had successfully done that in Jamaica, because the girls had no fears about Kingston, Ocho Rios, or Montego Bay, unlike many of our family members in the US who bought into the news hype and saw our island as not much more than a hotbed of crime that happened to have amazing beaches and life-giving foods. Marley and Sage walked to nearby shops without us. They made friends with children and adults. They climbed trees and ate new fruits, had sleepovers on the back patio, had long conversations with new friends in empty pools, eating mangoes and making memories. And now, with the support of one particular podcast listener through Patreon (a crowd-funding platform for creators to be supported by people who love their work), we took our first trip to Mama Africa, South Africa specifically, for starters. Those three months offered us so many rich new life experiences! Marley and Sage were resistant to the trip at first, feeling like they had no idea what they'd do in "boring Africa" and telling us they were willing to do this trip just once, to get it done and nothing more. Today, though, both of them will tell you in a heartbeat that they would live in South Africa long-term if they could. After we left South Africa, we found a small townhouse walking distance from the Pacific Ocean in little Costa Rican beach town called Playas del Coco. We were there for a little less than a month when Marley and Sage called a family meeting.

"We have an idea for a social experiment." Kris and I shot glances at each other as we listened to Marley and Sage take turns explaining their idea. "We want to go to a school for a year. Public school, maybe, or something close to it, but, either way, we want to find out how we would do in a school-y environment."

"A whole year though?" My eyes were darting all over the place as I said those words. My thoughts began dragging me through all kinds of muddy waters:

> Hell to the naah! Wait, what's going on? What's going wrong?
> Why do they want school? Is this me failing at unschooling?
> Oh shit, her mouth is still moving.
> What is she saying? I guess I should keep listening.

But ain't no way in hell I'm 'bout to. . .
Wait, I'm still not listening.
Shit.

"So that's why we think it's a good idea." Sage was finishing up, and I was nodding to fake-listen, while trying to get Kris's attention so that I could silently freak out to him through wide-eyed glares and serious eyebrow gymnastics and failing at listening to the rest of the girls' words. He wasn't looking at me, he was looking at Marley and Sage—and apparently listening, because he then started saying words, and I figured I'd better listen and hopefully gather some of what the girls said during what had become my silent panic session. I was so engrossed in the narrative we'd created and were living out, that of nomadic unschoolers, that all I could think about was how we'd be regressing into a regular-degular, boring-ass, school-centered, soul-sucking life, after these years of real-life learning and loving together.

By this time, Kris and I were full-time entrepreneurs who had untethered income-generating from geography, so it wasn't a matter of having to be in a particular place to work, but it still meant we'd have to settle into one city, make house, and, worst of all, sit on our hands while our children let the system give them things they would never use, all at the expense of their, and our—dammit—freedom. Logistics and resentment stormed all up into my psyche and overpowered any listening; I knew I couldn't respond in that moment, because the only language to which I had access was snark.

So y'all want to go get indoctrinated now? All of a sudden? After y'all struggled with all those emotions in school and finally got your dad and me to get y'all out of school? Huh? Really? Is this what we doing now? Volunteering for indoctrination and standardization? And I ain't joinin' no damn PTA either! That's what I know. And I'm not emailing anybody about any friggin booster-thons or cookies or candy sales or whatever. Them shits are scams! Yes, friends, scams! That. Much. I. Do. Know.

I said some of that in my mind and some of it out loud. Mostly, over the next few days, I slow-blinked, uh-huh'd, and brain-snarked, while I waited for them to stop saying words. I took it so personal that it took me several days to corral my thoughts, offer myself some space to process, and then go back to the conversation to actually listen and share the feelings that stayed after the reactive ones had time to show up, show out, and dissipate. It still took a few more days after that before I could actually listen, because I was still salty about their proposal.

And why'd y'all wait until I found $50 frikkin flights from here to Guatemala before springing this on us? Fifty. Five. Zero. And y'all know anything about indigenous Mayan cultures? Me neither, but we can learn about them in Guatemala! Did you see the apartment I found for us there? The patio? The rooftop deck? The low-low price of all that awesome?! And you still want to go back to America and go to . . . school? Maaan, this is some bullshit. That. Much. I. Do. Know.

When I'm upset, I need to feel like there are some things I know for sure; maybe you noticed that? That's an example of personal leadership. Not good personal leadership, mind you, just the broad area of personal leadership that I define as the ability to recognize things about yourself as recurring patterns and to recognize what actions you take based on those patterns. Now, if we're talking about good personal leadership, I see that as having knowledge of how you are, what tends to trigger you or excite you or motivate you. It's knowing yourself as separate from your thoughts, seeing yourself as the observer of your thoughts and actions and having a strong (beautifully imperfect) practice for responding instead of reacting to anything, whether that thing is a negative trigger or a positive motivator. And I think you can guess which area the girls' social experiment landed in for me, right? Yep: trigger, trigger, chicken dinner.

After nearly a week, I started asking the girls and Kris questions to help me manage my feelings and get back to a place of listening and expressing myself sans snark and saltiness. I began to see their proposal as a brilliant thing. Brilliant, because it showed that the girls could think of wild (to us!) ideas and feel comfortable sharing them. Brilliant, because we kept saying to Marley and Sage that our choices about how we live will always include them, and that their ideas about places to live, events to check out, all of that, were just as important as ours. I realized that if I stopped at my reactions to their idea, instead of tapping into good personal leadership, then I would be right back to the controlling, coercive, what-I-say-goes person I was when they were schooled children. I recognized my resistance as similar to my daughters' resistance, in that it offered something deeply valuable: a roadmap. I had long been saying that Marley and Sage's resistance is my roadmap, and now I was faced with the ways my own resistance could either root me further into my old habits or help me branch out into my deschooling work. These questions came up for me:

- If Marley and Sage really did own themselves, then why was I salty about them saying how they wanted to spend their time?
- Was I feeling threatened by them being in school? If so, why?
- Didn't I trust them, and us, to feel through the experience and pivot where necessary?
- What message would I send, what truth would I relay, if I opposed their idea without really thinking it through?
- Couldn't it be kinda awesome for them to experience being trusted with their own time and learning spaces by the two people with whom they need to have super-strong trust bonds?
- Did my rights as their mama extend to deciding that they had to stick to the choice of unschooling because it's something they wanted in the past?
- Did I stick to every decision I made in my past? Was this decision permanent?

- What am I really afraid of here?

Ultimately, we decided that Marley and Sage absolutely deserved to explore this option, and, if it was financially feasible, our immediate travel plans were to head back stateside, enroll the girls in the safest schooling we could afford to live near, and give them a year to farm their feelings in that sort of space. Turns out I didn't have to stretch as much as I'd thought, because we found what I now call an *unschooly school* right there in Atlanta, near my Mama's house, with a sliding tuition scale that slid all the way down to what we could afford to pay each month. That space turned out to be Heartwood, an Agile Learning Center (ALC) for families practicing Self-Directed Education, a space the girls and I visited a few months after I started *Fare of the Free Child* podcast. Learning about Heartwood, I was elated to hear that it was founded by a small group of parents and radical educators, one of whom was a Black man. What? A Black male educator who was organizing around Self-Directed Education? *Say word.*

One Year at Unschooly School

Our year at Heartwood is where I really learned the importance of amplifying young people's voices in the unschooling (and broader Self-Directed Education) movement. So much of what I learned was based on listening to Marley and Sage and the other children at Heartwood. This was the first time Marley and Sage were spending hours each day in a space that called for them to follow certain rules, do things at specific times, and be with adults who were in charge of them and a bunch of other children at the same time. Kris and I were so curious about how it would all unfold, and we were so excited to be able to support our girls' decision in this way. I thought Marley and Sage would last a couple months, tops. I felt the novelty of it would wear off once they realized that they had to get up at 6 something every single morning, no matter what time they went to bed (and they had no enforced bedtime by then), and that they had to do chores they didn't want to do, every single day. The structure of an ALC is one that sees students as partners in the space, and, therefore, just as responsible as adults (to the extent of each child's capacity, of course) to manage the space they occupied. This meant that children divvied up chores such as cleaning the bathrooms, taking out trash, washing up any dishes in the kitchen, etc. My expectation was that Marley and Sage would spend a few months socializing, and, getting tired of all the rules, tell Kris and me that it was fun and all, but that they'd had enough, thanks. I was so wrong. Instead, I got to witness multiple children, not just mine, see rules more like a rhythm to get into and conflicts as chances to have community discussions that (often) resolved things. At Heartwood ALC, the facilitators were not telling children what to do or how to solve things, they were nurturing the conditions for problem-solving, rhythm-finding, and creative exploration that supported the children who were there every day.

I first learned about ALCs when I met Tomis Parker who cofounded what has now grown into a network of learning centers with serial entrepreneur and self-described culture hacker Arthur Brock. Tomis reached out to me after hearing an episode of *Fare of the Free Child* and was later part of my reason for saying yes to a trial run with the Alliance for Self-Directed Education. In collaboration with famed *Free to Learn* author and committed SDE advocate Dr. Peter Grey and a handful of other people who believe in and practice SDE, Tomis managed some of the larger early projects with such an impeccable capacity to put the humans doing the work before the work. It was very effective in terms of our results, and, on a personal level, it was beautifully educational in terms of seeing how adept Tomis was/is at helping groups get to the underlying, unmet need behind an emotion, working at it in ways that didn't vilify people or their emotions but, instead, used them to invite agility and grace to our shared goals. I've never experienced anything like it, and I've been on boards and worked and organized in a variety of group settings in various capacities throughout my forty-two years. When the girls got to Heartwood, we saw that Tomis was, in fact, applying ALC tools to managing people and projects. These approaches, I'd discover, modeled so much of what my family had learned to do at home in different words but with same energy and same idea of looking past the behavior to the unmet need, offering language for emotional and logistical needs, and recognizing inherent biases and power plays and avoiding them, by opting instead for a noncoercive, partner-centered approach to addressing any issues that arose.

In addition to working together at the Alliance for Self-Directed Education (ASDE), I've also worked with Tomis and the founder of Charlotte, North Carolina's only (as far as I know) ALC, Nancy Tilton. Tomis and Nancy, along with their amazing staff and volunteers, host what I think the US Southeast region's largest agile learning facilitator (ALF) training program. Every summer since 2014, people from varying countries gather in different cities worldwide to attend these ALF summer trainings to practice and learn how to deschool in efforts to facilitate natural learning together. The 2019 gatherings saw twelve events in seven countries. Founders of ALCs, like Julia Cordero and Anthony Galloway Jr., who co-founded Heartwood, spend anywhere between three days and two weeks with parents, educators, and volunteers gathered to learn about and work through the agile learning approach. To give you an example of the agile approach to learners and learning, here's what one ALC's website says in response to an often-asked question: "Does your school prioritize certain academic subjects?"

> We do not sort knowledge into traditional subject areas, as doing so discourages learners from interdisciplinary thinking and exploring innovative applications they may invent. Learning is not about amassing data; it is

about making connections, deepening understanding, solving problems, creating, and sharing. Facilitators support students in exploring the relatedness and convergence of learning domains, both in school and in the world around us. Sorting or prioritizing traditional subjects is rarely useful from this perspective.

Cue tambourines! Whoever wrote that went ahead and summarized what Marley and Sage had taught me and Kris once school no longer owned their time and the majority of their conscious focus. All they needed was space to decide on themselves for themselves, to go deep into different self-chosen and suggested areas of study, only and always with their consent. They needed boundaries not schedules, trust not textbooks. They needed to practice leading themselves, so that they knew who and how they were by the time they were fully responsible for themselves. It was my responsibility to unlearn what I had believed about learning and about my daughter's rights and roles as children, and to recognize that the further away our family got from the massive suck of school or student, the more we were able to see each of our daughter's unique brilliant way of seeing things and exploring things, the less we needed to ask, "Sooo, like, whatchya learn today?" out of fear that they couldn't prove they had learned anything—or, worse, that they hadn't actually learned anything.

The schoolish lens was fading and the connection, the bridge, rather, between learning and the type of liberation I wanted for myself and for my children to define for themselves was, in fact, leadership. A sense of confident autonomy. An ability to navigate the world with a strong sense of self that includes compassion for other people, and appreciation of being part of various communities, contributing to those communities and others on purpose and in love. Confident autonomy also includes an awareness of their place in the world, as they, not the world, define it. It means giving them space to decide on their own interests and to decide on what to do to practice the skills that will help them to be more than students who become adults with an education. They were doing this once they got free from school, because our home life called for logistics like chores and generating income, and, as digital nomads, finding housing more than once or twice a year—those sorts of things.

At Heartwood, they got to broaden their lens to include people who didn't share their backgrounds, peers who would tell them exactly what they thought, whether they wanted to hear it or not, and a host of other experiences that happen in shared group spaces, for hours each day. During that time, I talked a lot on the podcast with other families who saw how the agile learning tools introduced children to language and methods that were meant to nurture collaboration and meaningful communication. And it was working, because they were running the space alongside the adults and using the principles with each other to create the type of culture where everyone felt heard and relevant to the goings on of each day. These practices weren't just for the children either, because they brought them home, and we used them to work through conflicts around chores or communication. We still use them today.

Chores became a thing we could discuss without it turning into an argument. Doesn't mean I still don't have to ask Sage three times to take the trash out, but the whole energy of the exchange has changed. Now, when she forgets, she's apologetic, not even a hint of attitude. She's on it. She stays on it, then falls off, like me with pushups. Only, my pushup issues only affect me, whereas her non-prioritization of taking out the trash affects the whole house. It also speaks to how she operates in community. If we reach agreements, and she accepts her role, then does she see how her undone tasks are unfair to whoever else has to do them? Sage and Marley knew about that firsthand from being affected by it and by sometimes being the one causing the strain on other people, so they understood for themselves, the impact of those choices. As a result, they stopped hearing our voices as nagging and started hearing reasoning. Our conversations got increasingly better, because all four of us were maturing, learning how to communicate, to collaborate, and to solve things together. We made and revisited charts for chores. I stopped telling myself that if I didn't do something, it wouldn't get done right, and learned that the girls were willing and able both to be consistent with doing their part in our community of four and to understand how to be consistent, without me or Kris threatening to take away things they liked or talking to them like they were people we didn't like but had to live with. We were starting to treat our daughters more like partners in many ways. We had money, and they didn't, and we could earn money and buy property, but, in a lot of ways, we were realizing that much of our own unlearning called for us to reimagine and redefine partnership, not just education, and that meant we needed to be examining how we showed up as partners, how our children were showing up as partners, and how we could learn to be ourselves together, which, once again, went right back to personal leadership. That same personal leadership that led Heartwood co-facilitator Anthony Galloway Jr. to go in a different direction than his post-graduate studies were guiding him toward. You'll meet Anthony in the next chapter.

CHAPTER EIGHT

Living Examples of How Deschooling Helps Us Cocreate the Cultures We Need

One of the benefits of producing a weekly unschooling podcast is that you get the real-life stories about the disruptions to the common narrative that school is the best way to prepare for adult life. I actively seek out other people and spaces where the damaging narratives inherent in conventional, coercive schooling are examined and largely rejected. This whole chapter is about people who get down like that—Anthony, Tamika, Leslie, and Monique—and I'll share how their efforts to settle deeper into what they needed resulted in the cocreation of learning spaces that give families more access to self-directed skills and communities.

Anthony Galloway Jr.

> As I started to read more and research more and learn about things—and I was doing research over the summer for a research program that I was in in undergrad—I started to learn a lot about the system, and I started to take upper level psychology, philosophy, and sociology classes, and I got to learn more about the problems that already existed, and so then there became a drive [for me] to do something different, to show the education system another way to do things. And I started to see my own story in the things I

was starting to research. I was starting to look at gifted
education and twice-exceptional students and looking
at minorities and gifted education and realized that I
could have easily gone the opposite route.

—Anthony

That's a quote from Episode 12, where Anthony talked
about what took him, a mid-twenties Morehouse College graduate and a grad school student and ignited such a mindset
shift that he stopped graduate school and made his way to
collaborating with a group of parents from a Sudbury school
(another set of Self-Directed Education schools) and Julia
Cordero, another SDE-minded educator, to form Heartwood
Agile Learning Center (ALC). During this episode, Anthony
shared a sentiment that many educators have echoed when
talking to me, and that I've heard and read. This push through
school to college is not only ineffective for many, it is also
harmful to numerous people. So much of the narrative around
success in adult life urges young people to go to college, with
the promise of a clear and realistic path to job security, financial independence, and personal fulfillment. But, as Anthony's
experience in the education system as both a student and an
educator has led him to understand, college, for example, as a
means to success and financial security works for some people
but is not useful for others. The dominant narrative insists
that every child can "make it" if they just *apply* themselves in
grade school and college, yet there are widely ignored issues
of access, resources, and risks that cause school systems to
target, label, and punish some children—primarily Black children—and not others—White children.

As an ALC, Heartwood operates with the core intention
of protecting children's free play and organic engagement
time. That protection includes an encouraging of intentional
learning, emotional intelligence, social justice awareness,
deliberating and participating in the creation of their school's
culture, and tools for confident autonomy. Parents of young

learners are encouraged to step into their own deschooling process. I'm in contact with several ALC founders who have invested in workshops and trainings specifically for the families of their young learners. Unschooling organizers like Maleka Diggs of Eclectic Learning Network and Dr. Sundiata Soon-jahta of the GROW Initiative have worked with ALCs and other SDE-rooted spaces to strengthen communities' deschooling skills around culture, race, identity, and dialogue. The collective work is done to counter the narratives about personal value being tied to academic achievement, without value for other personal and emotional factors, and young learners at ALCs are actively encouraged to engage the tools that can give them clarity around what they want to create for themselves and contribute to their communities. This is a huge part of what Anthony sees as a solution-oriented education model that he can get behind:

> The intentional culture creation piece that ALCs do is so significant and so important to me, because growing up, again, I'm after the A's, and so I feel like now... that I'm just now learning a lot about civics, and prior to now I've been so unengaged with politics, local government, federal government. I mean, I did good on those tests, but I don't actually know it, and I don't practice it, but when you're doing intentional culture creation and everybody's a part of shaping the society and being engaged in their community... I mean, I can't even imagine how these kids are going to be when they get my age, when they get older than that, and how active they're going to be in their communities and creating their communal agreements for their space and with each other and being attuned to their neighbors and being attuned to their environment. That's probably the most significant part about the Agile model.

I'm with Anthony on that. I saw firsthand how in less than a year Marley and Sage benefitted from using a social justice–minded approach to being in community, much like I'm finding my rhythm by focusing on a postcolonial parenting lens.

Mind you, these tools and practices aren't exclusive to ALCs; people have been practicing intentional culture cocreation forever, but it was groomed out of people through standardization that benefits capitalism. Tamika Middleton, my very first podcast guest, has two children who, at the time of writing, are twelve and six years old. They are lifelong unschoolers and have formed community through the cooperative, learner-centered, and self-directed Anna Julia Cooper Learning and Liberation Center, which she helped found, and which is rooted in a radical Black queer feminist politic.

Tamika Middleton

> We are a multi-generational, decolonized community of care, healing, and intellectual exploration where learning opportunities abound. We offer a space where folks can live as their whole authentic selves and in their full dignity, while being affirmed in their worth and held in a community of comfort. We are dedicated to supporting our children as they lead us into a world that is liberatory to all.
>
> —Learningandliberation.org

Tamika was also a panelist for Heartwood's second Liberation and Education Summit in 2019. The summit, first held in 2018, focuses on Self-Directed Education (SDE) and marginalized groups, SDE as a practice toward liberation, and creating and sustaining spaces for SDE communities. The annual summit is Heartwood's way of offering their immediate community and wider SDE communities everywhere dialogue and clarity on how social justice and SDE are intrinsically interconnected, as well as examples of ways to be deliberate about building social justice studies into self-directed practices and into all our relationships.

Social Justice Work

Social justice work is part analysis, part exploration. It is critical analysis of one's own practices and beliefs, as well as of other people and systems, to identify ongoing patterns of inequity, inequality, or bias related to a person or group's education, age, race, sexual orientation, physical or mental ability, socioeconomic status, gender, nationality, etc. that affect legal rights, health rights, and overall access and safety, followed by individual and group exploration of potential solutions to the identified problems.

The summits also offer families the opportunity to connect with families already practicing SDE, some at Heartwood, to share details about the ALC model and other noncoercive, liberation-minded approaches as a potential part of how a family can get involved in social justice work by joining an ALC and engaging in the topics, trips, and studies that link directly to social justice work. With her nearly two-decade history of organizing in social movements, Tamika knows a thing or three about deschooling. She is the Black organizing co-coordinator for the National Domestic Workers Alliance, a community advisory board member of Critical Resistance (formerly the Southern regional coordinator), a leadership team member of Kindred Southern Healing Justice Collective, and treasurer of the board of the Organization for Human Rights and Democracy.

> It felt very much aligned to think of what the power dynamics were inside of parenting, how we're replicating power dynamics that existed in the outside world, and how if I'm going to dismantle—if I'm spending my life dismantling these power structures in the world—what kind of hypocrisy or cognitive dissonance exists if I'm replicating them inside my home?
>
> —Tamika Middleton

Again, this is part of what I saw expand in Marley and Sage through their time at Heartwood. A lot of the unschooling children I know are very considerate people, and that's not because they are inherently *better* people than the schooled children I know. It's in part because they have practice thinking about how things benefit a community of people, not just how to stand out among groups of people to get the most access to the prizes/rewards of being exceptional—better than—other people around you. The classroom mentality, the schoolishness, extends beyond the classroom and shows up as inconsideration, which it often is. And when schooled children are not shining or appear to not want to shine, they are seen as unambitious or mediocre, and their self-confidence often wanes as a result. They come to believe this and seek validation from other people. For many children, unschooling has built their self-confidence, and, in terms of community, they actively practice skills for managing social conflicts, working through personal anxiety, not having to stand out to be valid, and recognizing how their own biases can be harmful to other people and how to do better. What we can do as adults is to recognize those schoolish patterns in ourselves and in our communication with children? How can we get more deliberate about our deschooling? We can start by asking ourselves questions like:

- Do I compare my children to other people?
- Do I want the children to do things in their lives specifically to make me proud? If so, is that okay?
- How do the children in my life feel about my presence in their lives? Does that matter to me?

Those questions are about power, and the examination of how power is perceived and used is one way for us to assess how helpful we are when trying to create community-centered conversations, and partnerships with children. And because life and, therefore, learning aren't linear paths, no single approach can be expected to work for all children, sometimes not even for one child. Communities like Heartwood and other ALCs offer one context and approach for self-directed community; there are others. Longtime educators like Anthony and Julia design and collaborate their way to creating exactly what they need. My repeat podcast guest and friend Leslie Bray cofounded Kid Cultivators Homeschool Community, another Atlanta-based collective that offers parents the benefits of group trips and regularly scheduled sports and other activities.

Leslie Bray

Kid Cultivators helps educate families on all of their options, including and outside of conventional schooling, so that each family can do whatever works for them, with support and in community, where families can grow together over the years, as they would if they were in the same school or classes over time. Sports days, proms, leisure trips, workshops, you name it, they organize it and make it accessible for their members. The structure of each child's day is completely up to each family, and Kid Cultivators supports that with consistent activities and education for making informed choices about how to go forward with their learning path, all under the umbrella of homeschooling, which, in this case, includes unschoolers, sometimes schoolers, and a variety of uniquely designed family living/learning models.

In Episode 110, Leslie talked about how deschooling for her has been mostly around leadership development as a community organizer addressing alternatives to conventional schooling. She longed for a community culture that wasn't telling families which educational model to choose but, instead, supported them in their exposure to and understanding of deschooling in learning spaces that don't put academic studies above human connection and emotional wellness. The logistics of planning a dual-enrollment workshop or an all-day sports event paled in comparison to the emotional needs of the families and Leslie's own needs as part of a small group of women handling all the aspects of running their "intentional community of life-learning families." Having been to a few Kid Cultivators meetups and having spoken to several people who've been part of their community for years, I can say that their space is a beautiful blend of home-schoolers, unschoolers, and no labels, just life. If you want to learn about dual enrollment for the state of Georgia or you just want to show up, talk, and make room for your children to show you what they enjoy, you can do that without judgment from the leadership there.

I first interviewed Leslie in Episode 18, talking about what it means to choose to do life together and be intentional about raising children with freedom in mind. As in her more recent episode, Leslie was clear about how things like social justice and self-care are major parts of a self-directed life, because if we cannot take care of each other, and we don't know how to take care of ourselves, what would it look like to direct ourselves and to lead children through our limited lens? The resulting efforts center deschooling, which I define as shedding the programming and habits that resulted from other people's agency over your time, body, thoughts, and actions. This is why Leslie talks about healing as part of Self-Directed Education, and, since meeting, she and I have had several conversations about the link between healing work and self-directed practices. Several other guests have also talked about how their own personal healing, not only from childhood wounds but also from baggage they had picked up in adulthood, really began when they transitioned out of conventional schooling or school at home. Their own healing began when they began spending time with their children and had the mental and emotional space to start teasing out some of the unmet needs and triggers behind the ways they interacted with their children. It became less of a luxury and more of a necessity to uncover the effects of the weight of the tools of oppression—physical violence, coercion, bullying—and they began to feel comfortable trying something different than what they were used to—like apologizing, allowing, or observing without attempting to solve.

These seemingly passive moves make way for deep introspection and simple daily practices that help solve years of daily arguments and resentment among adults and children. We start to recognize our trust issues, for example, and how our approach to trusting our children is often based very little on whether our children have shown themselves to be trustworthy but, instead, largely on the fact that we don't see ourselves as trustworthy and were taught we could not be trusted, especially as children. Healing is really at the core here. It's not about education; it's about relationships, leadership, being free to grow into our authentic selves together, and knowing how to support that type of freedom and growth in different relationships, personal and professional, at home, with ourselves, and in all our efforts. Here's how that showed up for one family and how facing it changed their relationship.

Monique Allison

"With this, you will face yourself over and over again!"

She had the universal mark my words look on her face as she explained how she had found herself going down the rabbit hole with the term deschooling:

> "I just feel like I have an overall understanding of what it is, and I can tell when it's happening to me or to Pharaoh," Monique's eyes looked upward and her shoulders lifted as she took a long, deep breath. She was reaching for the right words to convey how much self-inquiry and personal leadership work she was wading through since her decision to free her son from standardized education. "But," she continued, "I just feel like I wanna really understand it," she paused, "like, I want to be able to apply it to my life, not just notice it."

Monique and Pharaoh are a mother and son team who've been fighting together for all thirteen years of Pharaoh's life so far. His chronic illnesses make for a blend of regularly scheduled and unexpected hospital visits, sometimes as many as five a month. His sickle cell crises had been under relative control, as are the complications from the brain shunt implanted in his brain to manage the symptoms of hydrocephalus, but, still, up until about a year ago, Pharaoh was stressed and constantly frustrated, and the cause was not chronic illness, it was compulsory schooling. While we chatted during an interview recording, Monique talked about realizing that she was trusting her son's teachers more than she was trusting what she observed in him, let alone what he was saying. I am painfully familiar with that feeling. Marley had been saying she didn't want to learn at school, but in Kris's and my undisrupted schoolishness, we saw school as the place where children's *proper* learning happened. Monique felt that way too, so she (just like Kris and I did) handled it by spending more time with her son, helping him learn how to try and contort himself to fit into schooling. He insisted he wanted to be homeschooled, but Monique didn't trust that her son could make an informed decision about his education; I know just how that feels.

In 2016, Pharoah's ongoing petition for liberated learning showed up in his emotional health, not just in his words. He was stressed out from missing classes and overwhelmed with past due homework, all of this because of unavoidable hospital visits that turn into overnight stays and chronic leg pains that make going to school a physically and emotionally painful experience to postpone for another day. These stressors amplified Pharaoh's medical conditions, and his headaches were becoming a daily occurrence. He eventually went to counseling, and at eleven years old and dealing with chronic pain in his head and body from sickle cell and hydrocephalus, his primary complaint was school not his regular hospitalization for blood transfusions, pain management, or emergency surgery and not missing out on events with his friends because of his seemingly constant recovering status. His primary point of stress, in his words, was "having to deal with school." Monique learned, toward the end of their school experience, that one teacher was encouraging Pharaoh to keep up with his work by pushing through his headaches—which, in his case, are his body's way of signaling a potential brain issue. Pharaoh felt inadequate in school, and it was affecting both his confidence and his physical and mental health.

For some young people, school is safe space away from everything from mere boredom to deeper, denser truths. But for others, school is something to survive. And even though they might survive, the channels that open with school wounds stay open long after school years go by. The most pervasive suppliers of school wounds include bullies, hurt people in teaching and administrative positions, and security measures that target the boys and girls whose skin colors and stories are condemned through the imagination of anti-Black media. I experienced hurt people turned teachers, and was even suspended once for throwing my entire desk at a teacher whose actions caused me to feel physically threatened. Still, the impact of my school wounds didn't fully show up until I was an adult trying to make choices for myself. I realized how much my choices had been dependent on other people's ideas about the right path for me and how ill-prepared that had left me to confidently make big decisions about the direction of my life.

Eventually, Monique freed Pharaoh from school, and he enrolled at Heartwood ALC (the same one my daughters attended), an SDE school where stress and learning don't get sewn together like Frankenstein parts. Once Pharaoh got into a groove at Heartwood, he became more vocal about his needs, practicing his self-trust muscles and using intentional community creation approaches to education that make room for all the nuances of his unique personality and creative tendencies, as well as the layers of his chronic illnesses. He has voluntarily engaged in learning, especially culinary arts, and has participated in community food festivals through the school. He started learning how to be in community with

people who respect his unique needs, and who also hold him
accountable in the areas where he might need more practice.
Learning is fun again for Pharaoh, and Monique is learning
how to continue being a supportive partner to her son as he
develops and walks his learning path. Toward the end of 2019,
after Monique and Pharaoh made another important self-
directed move, this time to New York City, I asked her for an
update on their unschooling and deschooling processes:

> Pharaoh has a better understanding of what he likes
> and doesn't like and what works for him and what
> doesn't. He's more self-motivated and that shows with
> his commitment to his artwork. He sought out drawing
> videos, and from watching those videos he developed
> a few skills and sometimes draws without the video.
> When he comes up with an idea of what to draw, he
> gets very focused and takes his time to complete the
> series and has developed his own process. He's been
> doing this for about a year now. He interested in learn-
> ing about digital drawing and taking more classes to
> learn more about it. He's still into the culinary arts
> and watches his cooking shows. He started talking
> again about his interest in being a movie critic but is
> not ready to really dive into it. He's less stressed and
> always talks about how good it feels not to have home-
> work or have to work on school projects. He had devel-
> oped a stomach ulcer during his last year of traditional
> school (fifth grade) and since it has been treated, it's
> completely healed and has not returned. My two cents:
> that ulcer came from the grinding stress of trying to fit
> his unique needs into a standardized school system.
> He is more responsible and manages himself when
> it comes to recognizing when he can't push past the
> chronic feet pain and still go to the learning center,
> so he'll confidently say when he wants to stay home.
> He recently realized that the alarm he set for himself

to get up in the morning needed to be adjusted, and he made the changes, and it works for him. Since we moved here, and he attends an ALC here in NYC, he's met new peers that he wants to build a relationship with outside of the ALC, and we are working on that. He also maintains his older friendships through video chats and playing Fortnite with his friends. He's also more independent. He travels to school by himself and is learning to figure out his route when there are changes with how the train is running.

And I wondered how it had been for her.

Since we've been unschooling it's definitely less stressful for me. Not having to keep up with his school work and not having our relationship impacted negatively because of the pressure we were under feels much better. We are able to focus on the things that interest him. It feels good to go shopping for a set of markers that has the right red for his spider drawing, rather than shopping for whatever grade school supplies. We make decisions together when we are exploring resources that support his interest, so it's not me forcing him to do something I have in mind would be good for him, but, instead, we talk about why the resource can be helpful, and Pharaoh decides if he wants to at least try it out. Having the flexibility to schedule his doctor appointments without worrying feels good. I don't have to stress about his attendance at the ALC, and that he doesn't have to do any make-up work helps. Transportation became an issue, since I no longer have a car. But thankfully we are in a city that has a very accessible transportation system, and Pharaoh commutes to school on his own. It's not without worry about his safety when he travels alone, but we have a check-in system in place for arriving at school and back home or when he makes any stops to the store, and he follows it.

Monique will tell you in a heartbeat that this process has changed her for the better. She joked about how she had to watch out for her own tendency to judge people who were in different parts of their deschooling journey than her.

"It's so funny, I gotta catch myself, or I'll judge people by how they think about children now. But when I think about it, it's, like, I used to think like that . . . what, like a year ago?" She laughed as she told me about a medical researcher who had observed Pharaoh as part of a study on sickle cell. Monique found herself feeling uncomfortable with how taken aback the researcher seemed to be. "She said he was in full-out conversation with the doctor and the nurses, telling them, which shows he's into it now, and all of that. I'm like, isn't that normal? Isn't conversation just a human thing?"

Since deschooling is centered in her life right now, Monique's questioning of ideas and actions are a natural, healthy result of that need for clarity. Much of unschooling looks like shedding old ideas, including some ideas about how children and adults should interact. In Monique's case, she realized not too long ago that she hadn't yet shed a particular view of her son and would have been *all up* in his conversation, answering questions, filling in for him, not questioning whether that would be useful (or preferred) for him. His sense of confident autonomy was something she wasn't considering, and she didn't trust that he could handle himself in many situations. That particular deschooling lesson has been tough for Monique, as she remembers the lack of autonomy she felt as a child. A self-described Yes Child, Monique explained that she didn't questions things, that she was not one of those inconvenient people who rock boats. "I was always told what to do, and even if I didn't understand why, I didn't ask why,"

Monique recalled with a steadiness in her voice. "Yeah, I don't think I ever trusted myself to make my own choices," she realized, "because I don't think I felt trusted."

Children know that adults don't trust them, and that reality ensures that many children will simply perform for the adults around them, appease them, so as to stay under the radar and maintain some sense of autonomy. Monique's performance was unfaltering compliance, and that tendency, uninterrupted, and, in some cases, rewarded, followed Monique into adulthood. She writes candidly in her 2015 e-book *Releasing That Relationship* about how her childhood vices settled her deep into a seven-year marriage that, in her words, nearly broke her. Now that she's doing even more shedding and sorting, she is experiencing the ways unschooling permeates through to other aspects of living and decision-making and is helping her to cocreate the culture she and her son need.

> Having a son with special needs, for me, resulted in me getting lost in our relationship. No coincidence that the work I do outside of mothering my son is about exploring our own cycles of stuckness and working through them, healing from what they cost us. Even though school didn't feel good for him or me, we kept doing it. For me, once I was able to pay attention to the feelings, and the decision to do something different is now my work with relationships overall. The negative thoughts you have about your relationship are overshadowed by maintaining the look, upholding the conflict, keeping up the performance instead of surrendering to the necessary change, without processing it. That compels you to talk, to do something different, to put time or effort into working through it.

I'm feeling Monique on that one; there is healing work intertwined into unschooling—a spiritual aspect. There is no way that you can face your real feelings and real children each day and not come across shadows, spaces, vices, habits that you will have to reckon with, have to name and define and make decisions about, have to decide whether you will keep them or shed them, and if you shed them, what that might look like. So we know that unschooling calls for personal leadership work, and now we also know that it calls for us to do something that schoolishness absolutely stomps out of us if we ever had it: *trust*. Trust in ourselves and the ease of trusting people and emerging processes. Trust issues are, in my opinion, one of the deadliest by-products of a standardized, colonized life.

CHAPTER NINE

A History of Trust Issues and Ways to Leverage Language

Patois ('pa-,twä):
1a: A dialect other than the standard or literary dialect
 b: Uneducated or provincial speech
2: The characteristic special language of an occupational or social group
—Merriam-Webster Dictionary

Patois (pat-wah):
1a: Also referred to as creole or dialect
 b: Spoken in Jamaica as a primary language, along with English
2: A blend of languages used to establish shared meaning and mutual understanding among people
—Akilah

Society sees a child who questions authority as a child who needs to be reeled in by an apparently incompetent adult. A part of basic adulting, a widely accepted sign of maturity, is the ability to control the children in our care. Most of the people in any given grocery store, for example, cannot handle seeing a child be anything but compliant to an adult. I know you've seen the glares darted at children who mistake desire for need in public. Needing that particular food or toy and saying so out loud and with their body is grounds for a snatch up and calm down from a responsible adult. Children are supposed to know that they should always express themselves in ways that keep adults comfortable. That is among the many reasons parenting becomes our big presentation. Raising a certain type of child represents our extra shot at legitimizing ourselves to the outside world. We may have not gotten it all right in our own lives, and maybe we can't figure out how to fully trust ourselves, but, dammit, the children in our care gon' get *this work*! We may not have gone to the right schools and gotten the best jobs or lived the fullest lives, but, with enough care and discipline, we will make sure our children have a shot at all that bliss. Because we love our children, we invest in their education so that they can *win* at life. If they can just listen to us, we will support them by helping them not make the mistakes we made, giving them opportunities we didn't have, and pushing them to surpass us in education and economic status. We're not claiming to have all the right answers either. But we do know that we are smarter as adults than we were as children. We also know that there are many distractions out there that can lead our brilliant, beautiful children astray. We've seen people squander opportunities and use excuses as roadblocks to having rich, fulfilling lives, and that will not be our children. We are *not* about that Squander Life, so we shore up our resources, crook our index fingers, and bend our elbows, signaling our children to come around to where we are. To show up looking the way we need to see them. To secure the resources we give them with one hand and use their free hand to interlace their fingers with ours.

- What do we do about that?
- What might it look like to acknowledge that default lens and start practicing something different?
- How can we manage our trust issues without passing them on to children?

Maybe we can start by discerning what type of freedom a situation calls for. Because sometimes freedom is something we protect and preserve; other times it's something we design and provide. In a freedom-centered approach to parenting, so much of the work is in discerning between the times when we can provide freedom and the times when we simply need to preserve it. What I've learned from my ongoing deschooling practice is that freedom isn't always about doing, designing, or providing anything. Sometimes, it's about backing away—not to neglect or to ignore, but backing away so as not to impede or become an obstacle to a freedom that already is. When we are born, even as dependent as we are on older humans, we start with freedom. But as we grow from infancy into our talking and walking years, our history of freedom becomes compromised by expressions of love, by language, by lesson plans, by the lengths to which our loved ones go in their efforts to design *our* futures.

Adults tend to look right past who a child is right now, the present child, over to who they might become, the potential in the child. As that child grows into adolescence, adults still look past who that young person is now, and even who and how they were as children, over to who they might become. We trade in the present and the past for the idea of a well-designed future. We look ahead to the future that could be, and we discount that person's history of freedom. And our histories are important; for some of us, they inform our identity and help us define ourselves outside the pressure of parents and school and society. And even though I had my own childhood issues with schooling, it took becoming a mother to realize that particular connection between freedom and childhood. That connection between what I believed as a child and what I'm healing from as an adult. And that connection is basically a belief that trustworthiness is a characteristic of adulthood, and therefore was not applicable to me as a child, and the way that feeling of not being trustworthy, including not having trusted myself to make decisions for myself, affects how much I trust myself now, as an adult, to make choices without unconsciously, relentlessly relying on the need for external validation from a person I perceive to have some sort of power over me. The power went from parents and pastors and professors over to my supervisor or successful sister friend or somebody with more power who could give me gold-star A+ permission I needed to make a decision. And then the power passed on to me, not to use to validate myself but to initiate other children, mine and other people's, into this same unspoken order of subservience and please-pick-me-ness. In my attempts to work through this realization, I was guided by my daughters to start listening for a new language, to cocreate it with them as a way of understanding each other and deciding what safe things we can do when we do not understand each other and there is definite, fully acknowledged and embraced discord. I've come to call this aspect of unschooling *parenting patois*. Unschooling is a liberatory practice that empowers communities and families to raise each other and to resolve the generational trauma of attempting to force our dynamic selves into limiting and inherently racist, foolish, schoolish mindsets.

In our case, we partner with children to make space to learn about each other's needs without trying to force one understanding upon our child or becoming passive as we attempt to ease tension by trying to fit ourselves into what we think will make children happy. The functions of language include communication, the expression of identity, play, imaginative expression, and emotional release. When we look at the ways the children we love are either free or held back in their ability to communicate, to define and express their identity as it forms, to play to express their imaginations and their ability to process their emotions, we can begin to examine our participation in language-building—and assess whether we're involved in building it or are tearing it down or preventing it from happening effectively. So, together, each of my daughters and I create our own patois, our own language that fosters mutual understanding and shared meaning. And when we don't understand each other, we're learning how to use questions like our little translation dictionaries to replace anger with opportunity. Like when my daughter "gets an attitude" when I make a request, I ask what's happening instead of "checking her attitude," and I thereby discover underlying issues and root causes instead of reacting to symptoms and turning a moment into a minefield. The question is: How do we begin cocreating our partnership, our patois? We can use language to learn how to live in more liberating relationships with children, and we can start by understanding the purpose and functions of language. Unschooling is about mindful interaction and valuing human rights. The practice allows us space to shift back to Partner whenever we see ourselves veering over to Presenter or when we go from Guide and Safe Space Holder to Colonizer.

How do we access, much less maintain a circle, a community, grow a society where each of us, particularly the children we nurture, can be ourselves and bring ourselves to the societies in which we participate?

We do it on the daily with our language.

If we are developing a new normal together, what does the language consist of? Are we willing to commit to codeveloping a patois with each child we nurture?

If we are, if you are, I think there are some ways we might do that. Another of my most valuable deschooling lessons is the knowledge that I am bilingual in that I speak oppression by training and I speak liberation by choice. So, together, each of my daughters and I create our own patois, our own language that fosters mutual understanding, shared meaning. One way to support ourselves in the decision to raise free people is to acknowledge that language—verbal and body language—can be oppressive, and it can be liberating. And in recognizing that, we can explore our options for steering our boats toward more liberating language and away from the oppressive language we resort to when we're triggered. This is where patois has shown up as immeasurably useful for going from conflict to conversation with Marley and Sage.

What's beautiful about patois as I know it in the Jamaican context is that it preserves history and culture, while honoring the need to create something new that speaks to where people are now and what they need to communicate today. It's a newish mother tongue, birthed from necessity, fused together from other mother tongues, honoring what came before it, while making room for what is needed now. Applying the solution of patois to parenting calls for us to honor patois for what it is, our fusion mother-tongue, which will allow us to pull from the pieces of our past that resonate with us, while honoring what needs to happen now with our unique children and our unique needs. Patois allows for the feelings, the passion in self-expression, to come through. It honors the fact that people speak a language, and that the purpose of that language is to enhance communication, to bring people together where possible. The goal here, is to understand and speak our way toward less anxiety, less frustration, and less force in the ways we relate to children and teens. We are in a space where a new language is developing by necessity, and we can either let that language emerge and participate mindfully in its emergence through a partnership mentality with children, or we can try to force them to speak our language, to colonize them into something we might understand, mold them into something more convenient.

CHAPTER TEN

Patois-Inspired Solutions to Your Fiercest Parenting Critic Problems

Used to speak the King's English,
but caught a rash on my lips,
so now me chat jus like dis.
—Mos Def, "Hip Hop," from the 1999 classic album
Black on Both Sides

When Sage was about five years old, she fell in love with yoga.
I was reengaging my own personal practice at home, and as
an active *Mom Blogger* back then, I'd been sent a children's
yoga DVD to review. I gave it to Marley and Sage, and Sage
really enjoyed it. She practiced next to me at home, began
referring to herself as a yoga lover (there's a YouTube video out
there with adorable proof of this), and convened yoga class
with her grandparents as often as they would let her lead.
Of course, when this new interest rose to the top, I started
looking for a mommy and me yoga class to take full advan-
tage of this sweet new interest; certainly, they'd want to do
something fun like that, and it never crossed my mind to
ask them. Snacks, yoga mats, and extra clothes in tow, we
set out. We walked into the building and up the stairs to the
small, well-lit space. The floors were shiny, and the slivers of
light coming from the windows created light beams across
the flooring. All of the adults were women, and most of our
children immediately made their way to the light beams on

the floor, to skip or dance or stare at them. Sage was not one of those children. In fact, since we ascended the staircase and I first open the door to the room, Sage's arms were wrapped around my left thigh, and the more time passed, the tighter her grip.

"Sage, you're gonna get to do yoga today!"

"No, I'm not."

"Yes, you are, honey. This is the class I told you about. Marley, do you remember?" Marley didn't answer, because she was busy chatting up some parents behind me.

"I don't want to," Sage said, whining now, officially.

"It's okay, you can stay right by me, and you don't have to do anything until you feel like it, okay?"

"I don't want to," she repeated, and one of her legs was slowly following suit with her hands, wrapping around my lower leg this time. She was almost dragging the one unwrapped side of her body along mine.

"Sage, that's not comfortable," I groaned. "Can you let go of my leg, please?"

"I don't waaaaant toooo, Mama." Oh hell, it was now officially a thing. I could hear her voice lower to a quiver, and she was close to tears. Sage was not a loud crier; it was a low, constant whimper that both broke my heart and shot my nerves to shit. I picked her up, she put her head on my shoulder, and I walked out of the room, swaying her softly and asking her what was wrong. Her little mouth was in the shape of a perfect upside-down parabola, and her big dark eyes were wide and glassy.

"I don't want to. I don't want to." That's all she would say.

I kept insisting that she should want to, and that we would go back in there and give it a try. She did not let go of my leg, and it was an uncomfortable experience for us both. Marley, on the other hand, seemed to have had a great time, spending a good chunk of it trying to connect me with a few of the other mothers, so as to schedule playdates with her new friends.

That was one of many times that I pushed Sage to do something she explicitly stated she didn't want to do. It wasn't until we started and then stopped schooling that I began realizing that Sage did not need to be pushed in many of the ways I was pushing her. What she needed was for me to pay attention to her needs, to observe how she moved about, and try to help her get comfortable navigating the world and managing herself in alignment with her tendencies and needs. She needed the support and space to practice owning herself, to practice standing in her agency—yes, even at five years old. What stopped me back then from offering Sage that support and space is that I saw Sage's reserved, quiet personality just as school had taught me to—as a personal shortcoming that, with a little work, one could (and should) overcome. I didn't speak her mother tongue; I spoke mine, and I was groomed to colonize her space and acclimate her to mine. Unfortunately for Sage, it would be at least another two years before I had gotten familiar enough with the vital practice of mad question-askin' to see past my excitement about her new interest and listen to Sage's *actual* desires. Had I been in practice, the types of questions that would have come up might have included: Sage, I found a yoga class that you, Marley, and I can do together with other parents and children. Do you want to go?

Maybe I would've honored her saying no. Or maybe I would have still gone, even if she said no. But I would have paid attention to her reaction and maybe offered her something she could do without engaging with other children (read a book, do one of her puzzles, draw, etc.) while Marley and I took the class. In that case, I might've asked, "Sage, I want to go to this mommy and me yoga class, and you will need to come with me and Marley, because you can't stay home alone. Do you want to participate in the class? Or do you want to bring things you can do while Marley and I take the class?" Or maybe I would have gone on a day when Kris or one of our parents could have stayed with Sage while Marley and I took the class.

These are things I learned to ask later on in our journey. These are the types of questions that remind Sage that I do not need or expect her to perform outgoing or to do things she doesn't want to do. I don't find that this limits what she is willing to try. She is a very discerning person and takes her time to make a decision. I am learning how to trust that, how to respect that, and how to make room for her to practice being comfortable with herself, while still making space to stretch beyond her comfort zone, sometimes with my nudging. But because she sees my efforts to respect her choices and her process, she trusts me to know when to push and when to hold. There have been times, especially in the more recent years, where Sage made a decision to *not* do a thing, and after talking with me or Kris decided to go ahead and do it. That did not come from manipulation but from trust-based conversation. Sage sees Kris and me as trustworthy, and we also trust Sage, so our conversations do not hide our feelings, they state them, in a context of trust not coercion, and Kris and I work hard to recognize our inherent biases and listen to Sage as her own person and as our daughter at the same time.

Marley, in one of our deschooling workshops together, mentioned a similar sentiment. It was an online workshop, and one of the other parents also had their teenage son in the (virtual) room. Marley reminded us that children can and do develop trust and understanding in parents' experience. There have been several times where Marley moved from firm and adamant about a choice to curious and flexible after discussing it with Kris or me. This is an example of her showing us that she trusts us. We meet that trust with a commitment to listening, and much of how we do that is by constantly working to discern between our fears for her (as parents) and our capacity to support her (as partners) in gaining confident autonomy. When Kris and I allowed Marley and Sage to walk to local shops alone, for example, we were discerning between our fear and our capacity. We could have said that it was not safe, that between strangers, stray dogs, and a new-to-us neighborhood, it just wasn't smart to take that risk. While all those risks were real, what's also real is that they wanted to walk together, without us. They wanted to experience the uncertainty of the walking path, of choosing their own snacks, of completing the checklist of foods we asked them to get; all of that was part of their process toward confident autonomy. If we had denied them that walk, we may perhaps have saved them from all the variables that concerned us, but it would have also cost them an opportunity to feel comfortable and confident in their ability to follow a new path, to pivot when they take a wrong turn, to look out for potential danger and avoid it, and to come back home feeling accomplished and trusted.

Unschooling with Kris, Marley, and Sage has taught me so much about the power of observation. Slowing down to notice reactions, interactions, patterns, all of it, makes for easier access to deliberate choice. That slow down/pay attention approach works for many things, not just parenting, but, in this context, it taught me a valuable lesson: it's not *how* you parent that best informs your actions, it's *who* you're parenting with. And I don't mean the adult co-parent; I mean the child you're living with and parenting. Adding the word "with" brings consent into the picture, as parenting "with" means basing action off experience with your child and not necessarily experience with your childhood, paving a path you may have little to no experience with.

When my parenting experience went from being with an outgoing, very vocal, very much out loud type of person—Marley—to an "I'm good, thanks, and if I need anything I'll let you know" bona fide introvert—Sage—my parenting style didn't matter; the person being parented is what did. Turns out that parenting an introvert is not as simple as doing parenting stuff quieter! When we got to that yoga class, and she hid behind my leg the entire time, but at home we made videos about her being a yoga-lover and whatnot, I fell into the trap of schoolishness and plastered my parenting approach all over the reality of the situation. My schooled mind informed me that a certain personality type is what you want, and another (quiet, reserved) is what you want to avoid, and I reacted accordingly. School was my barometer in that moment, instead of Sage being my barometer for what she wanted or needed. Can you relate? If so, it's okay to feel shitty about it for a moment, but remember that guilt drives reactive parenting, so don't get so stuck feeling guilty that you forget your options for working through the situation or learning from it and making different choices going forward.

- Can you think of an incident where you may have put your approach to parenting or teaching before the actual child in front of you?
- How might you handle that from a partner-centered approach in the future?
- Is it too late to bring up that situation and use it to start developing your patois together?

This ain't comin' as news to you, but becoming a parent doesn't *automagically* equip one for parenting—similar thing with teachers and teaching. Training and preparation are one thing; the reality of it in real time is an entirely different thing. Likewise, having one child doesn't mean you'll know how best to parent a second one. Each of us, especially as children, have our own way of seeing things, our own lens, our own language, an internal mother tongue that will not share meaning with anyone else. It is built into who we are and how our early experiences shaped the way we see and need things. When it comes to words and non-verbal cues, there is language we observe and feel, and then there's language we are taught to employ. The language we employ, both verbal and non-verbal, is usually tied to power. In other words, whatever dominant narrative there is from the people in power about how we should sound and how we should present ourselves is usually not our mother tongue. Language can inspire comfort, confidence, and kinship. It can also cause separation and suppress real emotions. Start with seeing deschooling as something for you! Deschooling yourself is to explore yourself outside of coercion. Who am I? How am I? What might that look like? But before all of that, there is often a necessary pause, and deschooling is the first pause, the first outright attention to self-inquiry. For children, it's about how to own their time. For adults, the pause can help us move away from questions like: If we stop doing this, what do I put here? Then we can move on to better questions, like: "When I pay attention, what's showing up here?"

It's actively exploring who we are and how the things we connect with the most show up. It's about curiosity over control. It's learning how to communicate with your kid now that there's no series of liaisons telling you how their student status is going. Learning your children's body language in the context of curiosity through observation with your own senses, wondering what lights them all the way up these days. And it's making time to research and learn more about unschooling itself. It's very active, but it's also intentionally slow and steady. Your unschooling and deschooling practices will call for plenty of allowing, trust-building, exploring unschooling, and seeing it in action—massive engagement, very little control. Acknowledging as we do so that we tend to see control or attempts to control as active parenting, and, conversely, we see allowing and evolving as passive parenting.

Sage was annoyed back in that yoga class, and so she wasn't listening to me, and she knew she wasn't being listened to by me. That's not a five-year-old's issue; that's a *person to person* thing, a relationship issue, a trust issue. Sure, sometimes children do not understand the impact of the thing they want or don't want to do. Sure, sometimes five-year-olds are irrational and whiney. Sometimes, fifty-five-year-olds are irrational and whiney. Know any of those? And the same goes for teenagers. Now, as I'm writing this, Sage and Marley are thirteen and fifteen respectively. Kris and I field questions from folks about what is viewed as inevitable teen attitude and angst. Certainly, we have our moments of discord. I have my "why is this kid trippin'?" moments, and my daughters have their "why is this woman trippin'?" moments. Often, though, these moments are not at all about inevitable attitudes and the normal order of teens and parents. Instead, they are about learning how to be ourselves together by learning each other's current language.

Here are some of the tips Marley and I have shared in some of the communications workshops she and I host online and in person. Some of it is on us, which is great news, because we can do something about it. Some of it will call for us to show up as guides who are willing to push for what we think is needed. This is as important as making room for freedom. The other type of freedom, the kind that calls for us to define and design it, means that we are not excused from being discerning about when to push and when to hold. We cannot be so afraid that we don't push our children sometimes, ask them to prove a point they want us to honor, when we and they are at that stage together. This happens now that our girls are making travel plans, for example, that don't have to include Kris or me, because Marley is almost sixteen. For me, this means that I put the responsibility on Marley to inform me about the places she wants to go and to tell me what she is doing and how she needs my help to make the trip a reality. I want to know why and when and with whom. And I don't see it as my job to figure out how to say yes to supporting her trip but to sit with it, to get the details, to have the discussions, and to decide together. That is what I hope our trust-based partnership will enable, and it does (so far!). I know there will be times when we won't come to the same conclusion about a plan, and Marley or Sage will be at a stage or age where they can apply their autonomy and make a decision independent of my or Kris's approval. I am okay with that (so far!), because what they need isn't our approval but the tools to make informed choices about their lives, and those won't always make sense to me, just like mine didn't always make sense to my parents. If it affects parents though, as in legally, for example, then Kris's say and my say matters, and Marley and Sage have been alright with that (so far!).

- Is it always easy to back up and allow them to make choices I don't agree with?
- Is this choice an adult gaze situation or a healthy concern?
- Have I communicated my concerns to this child (not my frustration or fears but my concerns)?
- What is the difference between my frustrations/fears and my concerns?
- Am I comfortable that I can talk about this without crossing any communication boundaries this young person and I have set (i.e., if they asked you to only talk to them in private not in front of other adults, or if they asked you not to yell at them)?
- Am I still honoring the communications boundaries this young person and I have established, even though I am concerned?

When Marley or Sage aren't in agreement with us or us with them, that's one set of issues. But the other critics, the people in our lives who were also taught that they were not trustworthy and that children are inherently untrustworthy, they often call for us to bring a different set of tools to the practice.

- Are you gonna let him get away with that?
- This child is spoiled, tsk, tsk, tsk!
- She sure has you wrapped around her little finger!
- You know you should pop him when he does that, or he won't know any better!
- That kind of behavior only turns into one thing!
- So what if he doesn't want to do it? It's your job to make him!

I bet you can add some critical comments too, right? Kris and I have been fielding those for more than a dozen years now, and I can't really say I've gotten better at handling them.

What has happened is that Marley and Sage have gotten better at fielding them, and Kris and I have gotten better at managing our need to control what other people think about our relationships with our daughters.

For many, especially those who rely on extended family for regular logistical and financial support in raising their children, the practice of raising free people is made complicated and feels like too much of a risk. The unschooling approach, when extended past education and deep into the other aspects of adult-child relationships, gets plenty of criticism for appearing to lack the influence and control adults are expected to have over children and adolescents. One woman in my Raising Free People workshop, a wife and mother of one we'll call Naila, laid it "all the way" out when she wrote this after our session titled See Yourself as Society:

> [B]ecause [the parenting approach we develop for raising free people] rarely elicits the expected and accepted "payoffs" of immediate obedience, compliance, or remorse from children, that appears to prove that traditional parenting "works." Why does your child not do what you say? Why are they questioning you? Why do/don't they do this/that? Why aren't you punishing them for that bad behavior?!? [Those are] just some of the real and imagined criticisms I feel are levelled at me and my parenting style, which at times seem to point to my apparent lack of control and power.

What Naila is speaking to here is the judgment of her and the impending outcome for the person she's raising. Even more particularly, Naila is addressing the ways our society has separated consent from childhood and adolescence and replaced it with control and what it costs us to choose our children and our truths while managing these judgments, often feeling alone while we do it. And when we add the element of support from our parents, financial support, transportation to and from activities, shared housing, etc., it's not as easy or practical to dismiss naysayers. We sometimes need to educate them, or at least help minimize their anxiety by showing them examples outside our own family and connecting unschooling to other life topics, such as social justice and civil rights. Here are some questions I recommend asking them to guide them toward educating themselves. I've also included some questions for your own inner critic, in hopes that you don't surrender to feelings of guilt that you're getting it wrong and, instead, remember how to question your way to continued improvement of your raising free people practice. Let's call these counter-questions that can replace the critic's questions. Remember that this is personal leadership work seated in the context of adult-child relationships, so it would be a mistake to take every criticism you get and throw it at your child like you're throwing it at a testing wall.

Always be asking:

- Whose actual issue is this?
- Am I willing to put those person's boots on and stomp all through this relationship I'm growing with this child?

As for the rest of the questions, here are five additional counter-questions to get you started. Add three more so you have an even ten to grab and use in that moment when all you want to do is something that probably . . . definitely . . . wouldn't make the situation any better.

1. If you unschool, you can ask:
Can I give you some podcast recommendations to familiarize you with what we're doing and why we choose it? And, yes, I'm recommending *Fare of the Free Child* podcast and any others that cover those topics and help you feel connected and confident in your practice. Some unschooling podcasts are great because they:

- go beyond definitions and consciousness-raising to plans in action and new layers of work to define,

    navigate, theorize, and develop a deeper understanding of unschooling and deschooling;
- establish a sense of global community;
- help local Self-Directed Education–minded families and groups find and connect with each other.

2. If they seem to already be thinking about deschooling, and maybe even some of their own issues with school, you can ask:

Have you read the deschooling reading list? No, here's the link: http://bit.ly/deschoolingreadinglist. You should check it out. It gives sixteen detailed perspectives on deschooling as it relates to various aspects of our lives and relationships. One site calls it required reading for any beginning deschooling journey, and I recommend it all the time.

    This list of links includes:

- "Three Cups of Fiction. On 'Whites in Shining Armor' & the Toxic Fantasy of Saving the World with Schools"—Carol Black
- "The Dangers of Back to School"—Peter Gray
- "Occupy Your Brain: On Power, Knowledge, and the Re-Occupation of Common Sense"—Carol Black
- "The Trouble with Knowledge"—Munir Fasheh
- "A Thousand Rivers: What the Modern World Has Forgotten About Children and Learning"—Carol Black
- "Children Teach Themselves to Read"—Peter Gray
- "How to Eradicate Illiteracy without Eradicating Illiterates"—Munir Fasheh
- "McEducation for All: Whose Agenda Does Global Education Really Serve"—Manish Jain
- "Responses to UNESCO's McEducation Proposal"
- "What Is Education For: Six Myths About the Foundations of Modern Education, and Six New Principles to Replace Them"—David H. Orr

- "Learning? Yes, of Course. Education? No, Thanks"—Aaron Falbel
- "Erica Goldson's Valedictory Speech"
- "Democratic Education of an Unschooler"—Astra Taylor
- "Is Real Educational Reform Possible? If So, How?"—Peter Gray
- "The Most Basic Freedom Is the Freedom to Quit"—Peter Gray
- "Why We Need to Break Up with Schools"—Akilah Richards

3. If they enjoy computer time, send them to self-directed. org to deep dive into noncoercive, trustful learning environments, by saying:

Hey, have you heard of the Alliance for Self-Directed Education (ASDE)? Their website is great because it offers:

- free resources;
- deep research;
- established voices;
- local support.

You can also encourage them to embrace a diet of one article from Tipping Points (ASDE's online magazine found on the website) per week. These articles will offer them:

- a variety of experiences, backgrounds, perspectives;
- specific examples of effective SDE;
- insight into multiple aspects of SDE in family and shared non-familial settings (schools, centers, maker spaces, etc.)

4. If they're the data-driven type, suggest research on Peter Gray's Psychology Today blog, by saying:

Hey, I know where you can find answers to probably every question you've asked me about this choice we've made with (kid you love). On this blog you can find:

- scholarly journal articles on the value of play as the basis of learning;
- detailed explanations about the psychological wounds caused by compulsory schooling and potential solutions to them.

5. Ask them about their school wounds:

Invite them to share some of the ways they did not find solace or joy in school. Many people are really attuned to those experiences, and sometimes those conversations can bring them in touch with things they may have forgotten. Also, if your child's demeanor and mood have improved since transitioning out of school, bring that to their attention; let them feel through the emotional benefits and steer away from their perception of the academic benefits (or losses).

CHAPTER ELEVEN

Being Willing to Be Called In, and Out, by Children

"Why does it matter? What difference does it make?"

I had seen that face a thousand times before. Head cocked to one side, eyebrows scrunched up like she was looking at the sun. Marley was annoyed and unimpressed with the repetitive nature of this particular deschooling lesson she kept trying to teach me, nearly seven years into our unschooling journey. We were heading to a gathering with a few other families in our circle. Marley had a sweater and a pair of jeans she loved and wore most times we went somewhere that called for more than our super-casual everyday wear.

"You just wore that like three days ago, though."

"Yep, then you washed it, and I'm wearing it now, *Mommm*."

"I see that, and I'm wondering whether you couldn't wear a different top this time."

"Of course, I could, but I don't want to. We talked about this already, Mom."

Where was the lie? *Nowhere*. We had talked about it. And I had jogged around her backwards on my toes in circles many times before, just to come back to the left-jab reality that I was trying to get her to buy into—my performance techniques. She spots it and calls me on it every time, and I'm finally starting to self-correct. It's inspiring to me how patient Marley and Sage both tend to be with me on the small stuff like trying to get them to buy into social ideas like not wearing the same thing consecutively unless it's actually a uniform. It's so irrelevant, but it's clearly something I accepted, and then attempted, at first without realizing it, to pass on to Marley and Sage. And they wanted zero part of that bullshit and called it out a mile away, and they continue to do just that.

"Mom, I don't care if they notice that it's the same outfit or whatever." She had her hand on my shoulder at this point, forehead low, slight smile across her sweet face, obviously trying to speak to me past my big-ass baggage.

"You are so frikkin right. My bad, Marley. Thank you." Some version of that series of phrases have become part of the relationship patois that emerged through our unschooling liberation walk.

True ting. Deschooling Moment! My bad, Sage!

Oh shit, I get what you're saying! My bad, Marleyyy!

Rhaatid! No, I totally get that now.

Then I rest my cheek in my palm.

Then I feel really bad that she (whichever daughter it may be) has to deal with me not understanding something for so many years of our relationship.

Yooooo, I get why you're saying that! Then for, like, five whole minutes, I'm nodding my head real slow and looking around while the puzzle pieces come together.

Okay wait . . . yeah, yes! That would piss me off too. For sure. My bad!

Sage, remember the other day when you said. . . ? I get it now. I processed that shit, and I totally get it. I'm so sorry about that!

And our daughters really seem to get that Kris and I grew up a totally different way and need some support at times to live out the equality we believe in. I know they get that because of how compassionate they can be when we have those Oh Shit, My Bad! moments. Marley's same outfit situation is small potatoes, but in the moment it's another inch added to a growing wedge of disconnects between us. If we are not deliberate about learning each other's needs and developing healthy communication habits, our relationship will strain as we both get older. Marley and I talk about this, and she will even comment when we go more than a few days without getting into it about some boundary or task or need.

"You know it's been three days since we've had a thing, right?" Then she'll put out a fist for me to bump. And then I'm all #Motherhoodraisedme and floating around for the day! Marley and Sage are definitely raising me too. And what part of that upbringing taught me how often our reactions to our children's choices are self-inflicted, perceived wounds. Sometimes our children's choices shine a light on our insecurities—the way Marley's one-true-outfit approach highlighted my ridiculous hang-up about people's perceptions about whether our girls had enough clothes (I'm not even sure that's it—the shit is curious!). In those situations, our response to the feeling of insecurity is usually to make our child change their behavior and, therefore, appease our hang-up, whether or not it's aligned with our values and beliefs. In this partnership-centered parenting practice, we don't focus on ways to influence our children's choices; we look inward first. We check in with our own feelings to check for unresolved personal baggage disguised as responsible parenting.

#Confessiontings

My biggest parenting fear—and I've got a duffel bag fulla dem—is this: I am afraid of raising a version of my child that is comprised of all the ways they learned to survive living with my wounds and me, a person whose actions are influenced primarily by the vices they developed to deal with my baggage, instead of emerging into the person they were meant to be.

How about you? What, as a parent, teacher, or partner, are some of the fears you have about the lives of the children you love? Do you communicate those fears? If you don't, why not? If you do, to whom and how?

That fear that when my daughters are grown whatever healing I'm doing just won't have been enough to raise the "right" person is the very same one I'm learning to lean into.

For me, deschooling invites a lot of putting shit down (old ideas and beliefs based on somebody else's baggage turned mine), as well as facing some things eye to eye, like certain fears. This "wrong person" I'm afraid I might raise is really just my soul's way of reminding me that I cannot raise my daughters by myself. Specifically, it is my soul's way of reminding me that I must partner with each of my children in order to know what they need and how to best raise them. Anything else will never be enough, and I am clear on that. And you, as someone reading words written in celebration of the movement to raise free people, need to be clear on that too. You cannot raise any child without the input of that child. You cannot be the best teacher or guide for that young learner if you are deciding *for* them instead of *with* them. You and I must see partnering with young people as personal leadership work, social justice work, not just educational activism. This is bigger than that. This is about power, about reimagining it by taking it out of the context of power-over and applying it to our deliberate efforts to raise and be people who know how to share our power and how not to stand in the way of someone else's power—to deschool and decolonize our way past using the tools of oppression forced into our hands through standardization and forced schooling.

If we can accept any form of oppression, we are susceptible to all forms of oppression. That mindset is imperative in our efforts to raise free people, because we are retraining ourselves to spot the ways we participate in oppression, so that we can begin pivoting toward something more liberatory, and because we don't always feel that we can do something about big, bad oppression in the world, but we do sometimes feel capable of changing our own behaviors. Yet we can't change what we won't examine; we can't break free if we still taint our freedom waters with coercive relationships among the people we live with and influence most. This is why raising free people work is revolutionary. It's both pushback and buildup; it is protest but also pivoting. It's getting mad and frustrated and deciding exactly what to do to feel better and to live better, to not just fight against oppression and injustice but to facilitate freedom and prioritize joy. That is what I see and hear about from families that design and practice sovereignty and diversity of thought and a willingness to allow the best structures for living and learning together to emerge. Many families are working to end the pattern of children who grow up and have to recover our voices. Unschooling recognizes that pattern and seeks to disrupt and, ultimately, defeat it.

What to Pay More Attention to Now

I invited Marley to co-facilitate the 2019 version of my signature workshop, and, thankfully, she said yes. We did it virtually, real-time, and spent two days hosting intimate seventy-minute video gatherings, where Marley and I talked about what we were learning and teaching each other about effective communication and about being our authentic selves together. It was incredible, and the families in that virtual room were very attuned to their own practices and brought some great insights to the conversations we had. There was one other teen participant besides Marley, and it was good to offer space for intergenerational discussion around the types of things we got into. We wrestled with topics of discipline and power, pushback and powerful questions. We laughed about being willing to accept our children's rights to their own feelings and discovering TikTok sessions on the toilet. *Yep, really.* So I'm sharing thirty-five things that emerged from those intimate seventy-minute sessions, a blend of gems and disruptive bursts you can say to yourself, write down on your bathroom mirror, put in your journal, or commit to memory to help shore you up while you practice this work and align yourself with your decision to raise free people. Pay attention to these things not to the critics, to the fears, or to the traditions that never did sit right with you. Much of this came from Marley, and some came from me, based on experiences I had had with either Marley or Sage. Some came from the other families in the room. All of it is relevant and useful here. Take as many of them as you need; quickly move past the ones that don't speak to you. Use what you need, as many times as you need it.

What I Pay More Attention to Now

- I don't seek out equality in adult-child relationships, instead I look for ways to build equity, which can look a lot like a healthy friendship.
- I practice discerning when to push and when to hold. Sometimes when my attempt to connect is met with unresponsiveness, I should back up not push.
- Children will have a different lens and may not accept my views. This is okay, and I am learning how to give them the space for their own ideas to develop.
- Sometimes the discussion calls for me to do nothing besides offer context, if I am asked.
- In conversations with children/teens, I am mindful not to give verbal versions of long, persuasive essays. I always pause to gauge whether or not my communication is landing on listening ears or if I need to stop talking and start listening—or do something else.
- I negotiate morning routines where feasible, but I don't force children to act out roles in my morning ritual preferences.
- I do not take a child's attempt to ask me to respect them as them building life as a personal affront to me.
- I am open and comfortable with being upfront and saying what I need to say.
- I'm learning to be transparent about what I need and prefer. I don't expect children to read my mind.
- I ask, so that I'm not assuming, what respect means to each individual (adults and children).
- I ask, so that I'm not assuming, what partnership means to each individual (adults and children).

- I ask, so that I'm not assuming, what boundaries mean to each individual (adults and children).
- When I am using my voice to prioritize partnership, I am trying to find shared meaning not to prove why I am right and a child is wrong, even when I know a child is wrong. This is because I trust healthy communication to create safe outcomes.
- I respond with questions so I can learn more not so that I can bring the conversation back to my point of view.
- I am becoming more attuned to the body language that comes *before* a blowup and to recognizing the role I play in a child not feeling heard or seen.
- It's comforting for the other person to witness vulnerability—human emotion.
- I trust that honesty is good for self-directedness.
- I know that it is never too late to start building trust in a relationship with a child I love, and I am in it for the long haul.
- I'm learning how to just listen, rather than trying to *fix* anything—to let children be heard, so they don't have to defend their feelings.—Domari
- If I trust myself, I can learn to trust my child.—Jillian
- Note to self: don't let mistrust misguide you.—Jillian
- I don't parent or teach past any child. I see and value who they are today, instead of focusing on who they might become in a future I cannot control.
- My raising free people practice applies to babies and toddlers too, therefore I don't say things like, "It's just a toy, nothing to cry over!" I know and do better.
- I am learning to listen with a Disruptor's Ear, which means I am practicing listening beyond my own biases, so I can help foster trust and understanding.
- I am equipped to operate with the wisdom that the boundaries a child sets with me may feel uncomfortable, but those boundaries still need to be respected.

- I consistently practice giving my opinion to children in less confrontational ways, so that the children in my life aren't on guard before they approach me to express themselves.
- I do not underestimate children.
- I help maintain brave space for children to express themselves.
- I am always paying attention to whether or not children feel comfortable expressing themselves or are afraid of how I might react.
- It's so wonderful to realize that boundaries can change in different situations, and that trust allows for the flexibility that boundaries sometimes call for.
- I am so very clear that rigidity of rules does not support confident autonomy.
- It is important to know what's present for both myself and the child at a given point in time.
- I invite and appreciate the disruptors that are coming up as I continue my deschooling.
- I am committed to better understanding and managing my emotions in ways that are healthy for me and the children around me.
- I honor the truth that each child is a whole, full, feeling being.

There are specific skills that self-directedness strengthens, not only in the home but in the human. And when it is embodied by the person, much like in the way real learning happens, it is a contagion of the welcomed kind, a rapidly shared focus on communication, community, and structure. Because unschooling is rooted in self-directedness, it calls for and facilitates the creation or adoption of words and tones—language—that convey our desire to learn more—more about each other, ourselves, our topics of choice, and our topics of urgency. But more than offering language for exploration, unschooling helps us cultivate means of applying the language we are learning and the tools we are acquiring to working through the results of applying that language to our relationships. That list of things, the things to which I'm paying more attention, is an example of going from language to practice. It is specific and simple. It is easy for me to say whether or not I'm going in that direction, and, if I'm not, it nudges me toward something different that I can do in that moment. When I wrote down the twenty-eighth item in the list above—I help maintain brave space for children to express themselves—that was not just words, it was a directive. In a moment when I lash out against a child's self-expression, I immediately get the prompt of "brave space" from those words, which nudges me to be brave enough to hear uncomfortable things from people who need me to know when I encroach on their boundaries. I can use that, not just think about it but to decide to apologize or to stop talking in that moment and listen and to speak without centering my sense of woundedness. It gives us practice not just language. Unschooling is a form of healing work, because it about the decision to trust and respect children. It is also about us doing our own work, as the adults in the positions of power, to facilitate our own transformations from dictator to trustful partner and sometimes guide.

What will you do beyond this book to continue your raising free people practice? Let me share with you, as we close, part of my own practice. Promise not to laugh. . . I call it my *4D Practice*, because it includes four things that start with "d": a definition, a design, a doorway, and a daily practice.

The definition is made up of the words that you would use to describe a comfortable living environment with children, where learning and life are not in separate boxes.

The design takes into account the *how* and *what* of unschooling, as in how it works in your home or school or co-op and what work it is highlighting the need to do more of.

The doorway is what unschooling leads you to, the deschooling path, the root causes behind the symptoms that drew you to unschooling in the first place.

And then there is daily practice, the ways to engage in the direction of long-term positive change. The consistent actions that make sure that all the deschooling and necessary disruption are in the direction you want not the ones you fear.

What elements make up your unschooling practice? Can you name the ways that a child in your life or you yourself are healing as a result of your choice to be a partner to a young person? These are some of the questions we can use as guides while we learn and unlearn:

- Where is more opportunity?
- What does working based on what this/my/our child is saying mean?
- Where can I pivot?
- How can I be part of more useful conversations about partnership parenting?
- How do I want to feel in my relationships with children, and what am I doing about that?

Walk toward your answers. Refine your own questions. Listen to young people as you unlearn toxic habits. Trust that learning happens all the time. Find community for your raising free people practice—and participate. Learn yourself. Trust children. Keep on seeking resources for your child-trusting, anti-oppressive, liberatory, love-centered approach to parenting and caregiving.

About the authors

Akilah S. Richards is a public speaker and the founder of Raising Free People Network, a social enterprise focused on resolving the ways that unexamined experiences with bias and oppression disrupt the capacity of families and organizations to sustain cultures of belonging.

Bayo Akomolafe is executive director and chief curator of the Emergence Network and is the author of *We Will Tell Our Own Story* and *These Wilds beyond Our Fences: Letters to My Daughter on Humanity's Search for Home*.

ABOUT PM PRESS

PM Press is an independent, radical publisher
of books and media to educate, entertain, and
inspire. Founded in 2007 by a small group of
people with decades of publishing, media, and
organizing experience, PM Press amplifies the
voices of radical authors, artists, and activists.
Our aim is to deliver bold political ideas and vital stories to all walks
of life and arm the dreamers to demand the impossible. We have sold
millions of copies of our books, most often one at a time, face to face.
We're old enough to know what we're doing and young enough to know
what's at stake. Join us to create a better world.

PM Press
PO Box 23912
Oakland, CA 94623
www.pmpress.org

PM Press in Europe
europe@pmpress.org
www.pmpress.org.uk

FRIENDS OF PM PRESS

These are indisputably momentous times—the financial system is melting down globally and the Empire is stumbling. Now more than ever there is a vital need for radical ideas.

In the years since its founding—and on a mere shoestring—PM Press has risen to the formidable challenge of publishing and distributing knowledge and entertainment for the struggles ahead. With over 450 releases to date, we have published an impressive and stimulating array of literature, art, music, politics, and culture. Using every available medium, we've succeeded in connecting those hungry for ideas and information to those putting them into practice.

Friends of PM allows you to directly help impact, amplify, and revitalize the discourse and actions of radical writers, filmmakers, and artists. It provides us with a stable foundation from which we can build upon our early successes and provides a much-needed subsidy for the materials that can't necessarily pay their own way. You can help make that happen—and receive every new title automatically delivered to your door once a month—by joining as a Friend of PM Press. And, we'll throw in a free T-shirt when you sign up.

Here are your options:

- **$30 a month** Get all books and pamphlets plus 50% discount on all webstore purchases

- **$40 a month** Get all PM Press releases (including CDs and DVDs) plus 50% discount on all webstore purchases

- **$100 a month** Superstar—Everything plus PM merchandise, free downloads, and 50% discount on all webstore purchases

For those who can't afford $30 or more a month, we have **Sustainer Rates** at $15, $10 and $5. Sustainers get a free PM Press T-shirt and a 50% discount on all purchases from our website.

Your Visa or Mastercard will be billed once a month, until you tell us to stop. Or until our efforts succeed in bringing the revolution around. Or the financial meltdown of Capital makes plastic redundant. Whichever comes first.

Revolutionary Mothering: Love on the Front Lines

Edited by Alexis Pauline Gumbs, China Martens, and Mai'a Williams with a preface by Loretta J. Ross

ISBN: 978-1-62963-110-3
$17.95   272 pages

Inspired by the legacy of radical and queer black feminists of the 1970s and '80s, *Revolutionary Mothering* places marginalized mothers of color at the center of a world of necessary transformation. The challenges we face as movements working for racial, economic, reproductive, gender, and food justice, as well as anti-violence, anti-imperialist, and queer liberation are the same challenges that many mothers face every day. Oppressed mothers create a generous space for life in the face of life-threatening limits, activate a powerful vision of the future while navigating tangible concerns in the present, move beyond individual narratives of choice toward collective solutions, live for more than ourselves, and remain accountable to a future that we cannot always see. *Revolutionary Mothering* is a movement-shifting anthology committed to birthing new worlds, full of faith and hope for what we can raise up together.

Contributors include June Jordan, Malkia A. Cyril, Esteli Juarez, Cynthia Dewi Oka, Fabiola Sandoval, Sumayyah Talibah, Victoria Law, Tara Villalba, Lola Mondragón, Christy NaMee Eriksen, Norma Angelica Marrun, Vivian Chin, Rachel Broadwater, Autumn Brown, Layne Russell, Noemi Martinez, Katie Kaput, alba onofrio, Gabriela Sandoval, Cheryl Boyce Taylor, Ariel Gore, Claire Barrera, Lisa Factora-Borchers, Fabielle Georges, H. Bindy K. Kang, Terri Nilliasca, Irene Lara, Panquetzani, Mamas of Color Rising, tk karakashian tunchez, Arielle Julia Brown, Lindsey Campbell, Micaela Cadena, and Karen Su.

"*This collection is a treat for anyone that sees class and that needs to learn more about the experiences of women of color (and who doesn't?!). There is no dogma here, just fresh ideas and women of color taking on capitalism, anti-racist, anti-sexist theory-building that is rooted in the most primal of human connections, the making of two people from the body of one: mothering.*"
—Barbara Jensen, author of *Reading Classes: On Culture and Classism in America*

Rad Families: A Celebration

Edited by Tomas Moniz
with a Foreword by Ariel Gore

ISBN: 978-1-62963-230-8
$19.95   296 pages

Rad Families: A Celebration honors the messy,
the painful, the playful, the beautiful, the
myriad ways we create families. This is not
an anthology of experts, or how-to articles on
perfect parenting; it often doesn't even try to
provide answers. Instead, the writers strive to be honest and vulnerable
in sharing their stories and experiences, their failures and their regrets.

Gathering parents and writers from diverse communities, it explores
the process of getting pregnant from trans birth to adoption, grapples
with issues of racism and police brutality, probes raising feminists and
feminist parenting. It plumbs the depths of empty nesting and letting go.

Some contributors are recognizable authors and activists but most are
everyday parents working and loving and trying to build a better world
one diaper change at a time. It's a book that reminds us all that we are
not alone, that community can help us get through the difficulties, can,
in fact, make us better people. It's a celebration, join us!

Contributors include Jonas Cannon, Ian MacKaye, Burke Stansbury,
Danny Goot, Simon Knaphus, Artnoose, Welch Canavan, Daniel Muro
LaMere, Jennifer Lewis, Zach Ellis, Alicia Dornadic, Jesse Palmer, Mindi
J., Carla Bergman, Tasnim Nathoo, Rachel Galindo, Robert Liu-Trujillo,
Dawn Caprice, Shawn Taylor, D.A. Begay, Philana Dollin, Airial Clark,
Allison Wolfe, Roger Porter, cubbie rowland-storm, Annakai & Rob
Geshlider, Jeremy Adam Smith, Frances Hardinge, Jonathan Shipley,
Bronwyn Davies Glover, Amy Abugo Ongiri, Mike Araujo, Craig Elliott,
Eleanor Wohlfeiler, Scott Hoshida, Plinio Hernandez, Madison Young,
Nathan Torp, Sasha Vodnik, Jessie Susannah, Krista Lee Hanson, Carvell
Wallace, Dani Burlison, Brian Whitman, scott winn, Kermit Playfoot,
Chris Crass, and Zora Moniz.

*"Rad dads, rad families, rad children. These stories show us that we are not
alone. That we don't have all the answers. That we are all learning."*
—Nikki McClure, illustrator, author, parent

Rad Dad: Dispatches from the Frontiers of Fatherhood

Edited by Jeremy Adam Smith
and Tomas Moniz

ISBN: 978-1-60486-481-6
$15.00   200 pages

Rad Dad: Dispatches from the Frontiers of Fatherhood combines the best pieces from the award-winning zine *Rad Dad* and from the blog Daddy Dialectic, two kindred publications that have tried to explore parenting as political territory. Both of these projects have pushed the conversation around fathering beyond the safe, apolitical focus most books and websites stick to; they have not been complacent but have worked hard to create a diverse, multi-faceted space in which to grapple with the complexity of fathering. Today more than ever, fatherhood demands constant improvisation, risk, and struggle. With grace and honesty and strength, *Rad Dad*'s writers tackle all the issues that other parenting guides are afraid to touch: the brutalities, beauties, and politics of the birth experience, the challenges of parenting on an equal basis with mothers, the tests faced by transgendered and gay fathers, the emotions of sperm donation, and parental confrontations with war, violence, racism, and incarceration. *Rad Dad* is for every father out in the real world trying to parent in ways that are loving, meaningful, authentic, and ultimately revolutionary.

Contributors include: Steve Almond, Jack Amoureux, Mike Araujo, Mark Andersen, Jeff Chang, Ta-Nehisi Coates, Jeff Conant, Sky Cosby, Jason Denzin, Cory Doctorow, Craig Elliott, Chip Gagnon, Keith Hennessy, David L. Hoyt, Simon Knapus, Ian MacKaye, Tomas Moniz, Zappa Montag, Raj Patel, Jeremy Adam Smith, Jason Sperber, Burke Stansbury, Shawn Taylor, Tata, Jeff West, and Mark Whiteley.

"**Rad Dad** *gives voice to egalitarian parenting and caregiving by men in a truly radical fashion, with its contributors challenging traditional norms of what it means to be a father and subverting paradigms, while making you laugh in the process. With its thoughtful and engaging stories on topics like birth, stepfathering, gender, politics, pop culture, and the challenges of kids growing older, this collection of essays and interviews is a compelling addition to books on fatherhood.*"
—Jennifer Silverman, co-editor, *My Baby Rides the Short Bus: The Unabashedly Human Experience of Raising Kids with Disabilities*

Parenting without God: How to Raise Moral, Ethical, and Intelligent Children, Free from Religious Dogma, Second Edition

Dan Arel
with a Foreword by Jessica Mills

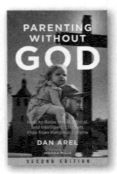

ISBN: 978-1-62963-708-2
$15.95   176 pages

Children inevitably turn to their parents for more than just food and security; equally important are assurance, recognition, and interpretation of life. A child develops best in an environment where creativity and discovery are unimpeded by the artificial restrictions of blind faith and dogmatic belief. *Parenting without God* is for parents, and future parents, who lack belief in a god and who are seeking guidance on raising freethinkers and social-justice-aware children in a nation where public dialogue has been controlled by the Christian Right.

Dan Arel, activist and critically acclaimed author, has penned a magnificently practical guide to help parents provide their children with the intellectual tools for standing up to attempts at religious proselytization, whether by teachers, coaches, friends, or even other family members. *Parenting without God* is also for the parent activist who is trying to make the world a better place for all children by first educating their own children about racism, sexism, and all forms of discrimination that continue to serve as a barrier to the fundamentals of human dignity and democracy. It's for parents who wish for their children to question everything and to learn how to reach their own conclusions based on verifiable evidence and reason. Above all, Arel makes the penetrating argument that parents should lead by example— both by speaking candidly about the importance of secularism and by living an openly and unabashedly secular life.

Parenting without God is written with humility, compassion, and understanding. Dan Arel's writing style is refreshingly lucid and conveys the unmistakable impression of a loving father dedicated to redefining the role of parenthood so that it also includes the vitally important task of nurturing every child's latent human impulse for freedom and autonomy. This second edition has been expanded with new material from the author.

Anarchist Pedagogies: Collective Actions, Theories, and Critical Reflections on Education

Edited by Robert H. Haworth
with an afterword by Allan Antliff

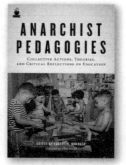

ISBN: 978-1-60486-484-7
$24.95   352 pages

Education is a challenging subject for anarchists. Many are critical about working within a state-run education system that is embedded in hierarchical, standardized, and authoritarian structures. Numerous individuals and collectives envision the creation of counterpublics or alternative educational sites as possible forms of resistance, while other anarchists see themselves as "saboteurs" within the public arena— believing that there is a need to contest dominant forms of power and educational practices from multiple fronts. Of course, if anarchists agree that there are no blueprints for education, the question remains, in what dynamic and creative ways can we construct nonhierarchical, anti-authoritarian, mutual, and voluntary educational spaces?

Contributors to this edited volume engage readers in important and challenging issues in the area of anarchism and education. From Francisco Ferrer's modern schools in Spain and the Work People's College in the United States, to contemporary actions in developing "free skools" in the U.K. and Canada, to direct-action education such as learning to work as a "street medic" in the protests against neoliberalism, the contributors illustrate the importance of developing complex connections between educational theories and collective actions. Anarchists, activists, and critical educators should take these educational experiences seriously as they offer invaluable examples for potential teaching and learning environments outside of authoritarian and capitalist structures. Major themes in the volume include: learning from historical anarchist experiments in education, ways that contemporary anarchists create dynamic and situated learning spaces, and finally, critically reflecting on theoretical frameworks and educational practices. Contributors include: David Gabbard, Jeffery Shantz, Isabelle Fremeaux & John Jordan, Abraham P. DeLeon, Elsa Noterman, Andre Pusey, Matthew Weinstein, Alex Khasnabish, and many others.

Out of the Ruins: The Emergence of Radical Informal Learning Spaces

Edited by Robert H. Haworth and John M. Elmore

ISBN: 978-1-62963-239-1
$24.95   288 pages

OUT OF THE RUINS
*The Emergence of
Radical Informal Learning Spaces*

Edited by Robert H. Haworth & John M. Elmore

Contemporary educational practices and policies across the world are heeding the calls of Wall Street for more corporate control, privatization, and standardized accountability. There are definite shifts and movements towards more capitalist interventions of efficiency and an adherence to market fundamentalist values within the sphere of public education. In many cases, educational policies are created to uphold and serve particular social, political, and economic ends. Schools, in a sense, have been tools to reproduce hierarchical, authoritarian, and hyper-individualistic models of social order. From the industrial era to our recent expansion of the knowledge economy, education has been at the forefront of manufacturing and exploiting particular populations within our society.

The important news is that emancipatory educational practices are emerging. Many are emanating outside the constraints of our dominant institutions and are influenced by more participatory and collective actions. In many cases, these alternatives have been undervalued or even excluded within the educational research. From an international perspective, some of these radical informal learning spaces are seen as a threat by many failed states and corporate entities.

Out of the Ruins sets out to explore and discuss the emergence of alternative learning spaces that directly challenge the pairing of public education with particular dominant capitalist and statist structures. The authors construct philosophical, political, economic and social arguments that focus on radical informal learning as a way to contest efforts to commodify and privatize our everyday educational experiences. The major themes include the politics of learning in our formal settings, constructing new theories on our informal practices, collective examples of how radical informal learning practices and experiences operate, and how individuals and collectives struggle to share these narratives within and outside of institutions.

Haste to Rise: A Remarkable Experience of Black Education during Jim Crow

David Pilgrim & Franklin Hughes
with a Preface by David Eisler

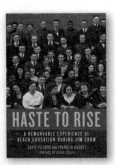

ISBN: 978-1-62963-790-7
$20.00   224 pages

Between 1910 and the mid-1920s, more than sixty black students from the South bravely traveled north to Ferris Institute, a small, mostly white school in Big Rapids, Michigan. They came to enroll in college programs and college preparatory courses— and to escape, if only temporarily, the daily and ubiquitous indignities suffered under the Jim Crow racial hierarchy. They excelled in their studies and became accomplished in their professional fields. Many went on to both ignite and help lead the explosive civil rights movement. Very few people know their stories—until now.

Haste to Rise is a book about the incredible resilience and breathtaking accomplishments of those students. It was written to unearth, contextualize, and share their stories and important lessons with this generation. Along the way we are introduced to dozens of these Jim Crow-era students, including the first African American to win a case before the U.S. Supreme Court, Belford Lawson, the lead attorney in *New Negro Alliance v. Sanitary Grocery Co.* (1938), a landmark court battle that safeguarded the right to picket. We also meet one of Lawson's contemporaries, Percival L. Prattis, a pioneering journalist and influential newspaper executive. In 1947, he became the first African American news correspondent admitted to the U.S. House and Senate press galleries. There is also an in-depth look into the life and work of the institute's founder, Woodbridge Nathan Ferris, a racial justice pioneer who created educational opportunities for women, international students, and African Americans.

Haste to Rise is a challenge to others to look beyond a university's official history and seek a more complete knowledge of its past. This is American history done right!

"One of the most important contributions to the study of American history that I have ever experienced."
—Henry Louis Gates Jr., director of the W.E.B. Du Bois Institute for African American Research

Anarchism and Education: A Philosophical Perspective

Judith Suissa

ISBN: 978-1-60486-114-3
$19.95   184 pages

While there have been historical accounts
of the anarchist school movement, there has
been no systematic work on the philosophical
underpinnings of anarchist educational ideas—
until now.

Anarchism and Education offers a philosophical account of the neglected
tradition of anarchist thought on education. Although few anarchist
thinkers wrote systematically on education, this analysis is based largely
on a reconstruction of the educational thought of anarchist thinkers
gleaned from their various ethical, philosophical, and popular writings.
Primarily drawing on the work of the nineteenth-century anarchist
theorists such as Bakunin, Kropotkin, and Proudhon, the book also
covers twentieth-century anarchist thinkers such as Noam Chomsky,
Paul Goodman, Daniel Guérin, and Colin Ward.

This original work will interest philosophers of education and
educationalist thinkers as well as those with a general interest in
anarchism.

*"This is an excellent book that deals with important issues through the lens of
anarchist theories and practices of education . . . The book tackles a number
of issues that are relevant to anybody who is trying to come to terms with
the philosophy of education."*
—Higher Education Review

Anarchist Education and the Modern School: A Francisco Ferrer Reader

Francisco Ferrer
Edited by Mark Bray and
Robert H. Haworth

ISBN: 978-1-62963-509-5
$24.95   352 pages

On October 13, 1909, Francisco Ferrer, the
notorious Catalan anarchist educator and founder of the Modern School,
was executed by firing squad. The Spanish government accused him
of masterminding the Tragic Week rebellion, while the transnational
movement that emerged in his defense argued that he was simply
the founder of the groundbreaking Modern School of Barcelona. Was
Ferrer a ferocious revolutionary, an ardently nonviolent pedagogue, or
something else entirely?

Anarchist Education and the Modern School is the first historical reader to
gather together Ferrer's writings on rationalist education, revolutionary
violence, and the general strike (most translated into English for the
first time) and put them into conversation with the letters, speeches,
and articles of his comrades, collaborators, and critics to show that the
truth about the founder of the Modern School was far more complex
than most of his friends or enemies realized. Francisco Ferrer navigated
a tempestuous world of anarchist assassins, radical republican
conspirators, anticlerical rioters, and freethinking educators to establish
the legendary Escuela Moderna and the Modern School movement that
his martyrdom propelled around the globe.

"A thorough and balanced collection of the writings of the doyen of myriad
horizontal educational projects in Spain and more still across the world.
Equally welcome are the well-researched introduction and the afterword
that underline both the multiplicity of anarchist perspectives on education
and social transformation and the complexity of Ferrer's thinking."
—Chris Ealham, author of *Living Anarchism: Jose Peirats and the Spanish*
Anarcho-Syndicalist Movement

*Teaching Resistance:
Radicals, Revolutionaries,
and Cultural Subversives in
the Classroom*

Edited by John Mink

ISBN: 978-1-62963-709-9
$24.95   416 pages

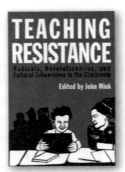

Teaching Resistance is a collection of the
voices of activist educators from around the world who engage inside
and outside the classroom from pre-kindergarten to university and
emphasize teaching radical practice from the field. Written in accessible
language, this book is for anyone who wants to explore new ways to
subvert educational systems and institutions, collectively transform
educational spaces, and empower students and other teachers to fight
for genuine change. Topics include community self-defense, Black
Lives Matter and critical race theory, intersections between punk/DIY
subculture and teaching, ESL, anarchist education, Palestinian resistance,
trauma, working-class education, prison teaching, the resurgence
of (and resistance to) the Far Right, special education, antifascist
pedagogies, and more.

Edited by social studies teacher, author, and punk musician John Mink,
the book features expanded entries from the monthly column in the
politically insurgent punk magazine *Maximum Rocknroll*, plus new works
and extensive interviews with subversive educators. Contributing
teachers include Michelle Cruz Gonzales, Dwayne Dixon, Martín
Sorrondeguy, Alice Bag, Miriam Klein Stahl, Ron Scapp, Kadijah Means,
Mimi Nguyen, Murad Tamini, Yvette Felarca, Jessica Mills, and others, all
of whom are unified against oppression and readily use their classrooms
to fight for human liberation, social justice, systemic change, and true
equality.

Royalties will be donated to Teachers 4 Social Justice: t4sj.org

"**Teaching Resistance** *brings us the voices of activist educators who are
fighting back inside and outside of the classroom. The punk rock spirit of
this collection of concise, hard-hitting essays is bound to stir up trouble.*"
—Mark Bray, historian, author of *Antifa: The Anti-Fascist Handbook* and
coeditor of *Anarchist Education and the Modern School: A Francisco Ferrer
Reader*

Understanding Jim Crow: Using Racist Memorabilia to Teach Tolerance and Promote Social Justice

David Pilgrim with a foreword by Henry Louis Gates Jr.

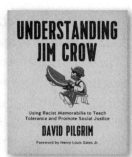

ISBN: 978-1-62963-114-1
$24.95   208 pages

For many people, especially those who came of age after landmark civil rights legislation was passed, it is difficult to understand what it was like to be an African American living under Jim Crow segregation in the United States. Most young Americans have little or no knowledge about restrictive covenants, literacy tests, poll taxes, lynchings, and other oppressive features of the Jim Crow racial hierarchy. Even those who have some familiarity with the period may initially view racist segregation and injustices as mere relics of a distant, shameful past. A a proper understanding of race relations in this country must include a solid knowledge of Jim Crow—how it emerged, what it was like, how it ended, and its impact on the culture.

Understanding Jim Crow introduces readers to the Jim Crow Museum of Racist Memorabilia, a collection of more than ten thousand contemptible collectibles that are used to engage visitors in intense and intelligent discussions about race, race relations, and racism. The items are offensive. They were meant to be offensive. The items in the Jim Crow Museum served to dehumanize blacks and legitimized patterns of prejudice, discrimination, and segregation.

Using racist objects as teaching tools seems counterintuitive—and, quite frankly, needlessly risky. Many Americans are already apprehensive discussing race relations, especially in settings where their ideas are challenged. The museum and this book exist to help overcome our collective trepidation and reluctance to talk about race. Fully illustrated, and with context provided by the museum's founder and director David Pilgrim, *Understanding Jim Crow* is both a grisly tour through America's past and an auspicious starting point for racial understanding and healing.

"One of the most important contributions to the study of American history that I have ever experienced."
—Henry Louis Gates Jr., director of the W.E.B. Du Bois Institute for African American Research

Watermelons, Nooses, and Straight Razors: Stories from the Jim Crow Museum

Author: David Pilgrim with a Foreword by Debby Irving

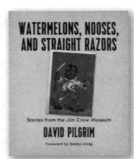

ISBN: 978-1-62963-437-1
$24.95   272 pages

All groups tell stories, but some groups have the power to impose their stories on others, to label others, stigmatize others, paint others as undesirables—and to have these stories presented as scientific fact, God's will, or wholesome entertainment. *Watermelons, Nooses, and Straight Razors* examines the origins and significance of several longstanding antiblack stories and the caricatures and stereotypes that support them. Here readers will find representations of the lazy, childlike Sambo, the watermelon-obsessed pickaninny, the buffoonish minstrel, the subhuman savage, the loyal and contented mammy and Tom, and the menacing, razor-toting coon and brute.

Malcolm X and James Baldwin both refused to eat watermelon in front of white people. They were aware of the jokes and other stories about African Americans stealing watermelons, fighting over watermelons, even being transformed into watermelons. Did racial stories influence the actions of white fraternities and sororities who dressed in blackface and mocked black culture, or employees who hung nooses in their workplaces? What stories did the people who refer to Serena Williams and other dark-skinned athletes as apes or baboons hear? Is it possible that a white South Carolina police officer who shot a fleeing black man had never heard stories about scary black men with straight razors or other weapons? Antiblack stories still matter.

Watermelons, Nooses, and Straight Razors uses images from the Jim Crow Museum, the nation's largest publicly accessible collection of racist objects. These images are evidence of the social injustice that Martin Luther King Jr. referred to as "a boil that can never be cured so long as it is covered up but must be exposed to the light of human conscience and the air of national opinion before it can be cured." Each chapter concludes with a story from the author's journey, challenging the integrity of racial narratives.